Giuseppe's Italian Bakes

Over 60
Classic Cakes,
Desserts
& Savoury
Bakes

Giuseppe
Dell'Anno

Photography by Matt Russell

Hardie Grant
QUADRILLE

Cakes & Tarts
Part 1

Small & Sweet
Part 2

Savoury Bakes
Part 3

Basics
Part 4

What's in this book?

When I set out to write this book, my ambition was to collect as broad a set of timeless Italian classics as possible, using my dad's notes as guidance and inspiration. But I quickly realised that a single book was only going to scratch the surface of the vast wealth of Italian culinary heritage, and I had to force myself to select only those recipes that I felt particularly close to. The result is a collection of simple and effective home bakes, deliberately designed to be accessible to the most inexperienced baker as well as to those who have already been baking for a while.

Where possible, I have tried to provide options to custom-build the bake with a modular structure, where the casing and the fillings are picked independently and combined freely. The ingredients are hardly exotic; they are mostly dictated by what used to populate pantries back in the day. Some might require some googling to be sourced outside of Italy, but they should all be available to most.

As is often the case when bakes are made out of very mundane ingredients, the success of the bake is all in the method. I have tried to be as precise and specific as possible in describing the steps: my proverbial pedantry will probably come across in the accuracy of measurements and temperatures given. The trickiest passages in the methods, especially those that require specific shaping techniques, are supported by video examples linked through the QR codes at the end of the recipe.

If the ingredients are simple, the history behind these recipes is always long and often controversial. Most bakes boast a collection of theories about their origins, birthplaces or the meaning of their names... I have deliberately stayed out of the debate, after all the only thing that really matters is how delicious they taste!

WHAT'S IN THIS BOOK?

Are these recipes truly authentic?

Foreigners refer to Italian cuisine as if there was only one, recognised across the country and acknowledged as such. The reality is that there are many Italian cuisines: one per region, one per city, one per family even. Italy as we know it today, is only just over 160 years old; in fact, some of the recipes in this book are older than that! What we refer to today as Italian cuisine is in reality an eclectic concoction of dishes originating from different cultures, a range of external influences, various climates and ever changing needs. And Italians relish such diversity: towns that are literally five miles apart will take pride and pleasure in boasting their own peculiar and individual dishes, even though sometimes the only difference is in the names...

Try to walk around the beautiful town of Siena and ask ten people for the original recipe of *ricciarelli*. You will probably get ten different answers: each *nonna* or *nonno* baking those biscuits in their kitchen will have perfected the recipe to their own taste and will be ready to swear that their recipe is better than the next door neighbour's.

So, how can I be sure that the recipes in this book are authentic? Well, I can't. Authenticity is an elusive concept at the best of times and all

I can offer here is my partial but respectful view of the recipes that I have gathered by travelling around Italy and by delving into the treasure trove that is my dad's stack of notes. Although I have refrained from being overly creative, at times I had to use my own judgement to pick one 'original version' over another.

My aspiration is to hand over to you my subjective interpretation of what I believe are authentic Italian bakes and, to do so, I have deliberately stepped aside and forced myself not to change any detail of the recipes I have captured. I have tried to be as accurate and precise with measurements, shapes and flavours as I can, to present you a bake that is as close as possible to what I have experienced as 'the real thing'.

My guiding principle throughout my research was to respect those recipes and avoid the temptation of adjusting them to what a foreign audience would consider palatable today. But that does not mean that you should too: do not be afraid of experimenting. Play with these recipes – change the shapes, rearrange the combinations, adjust the flavours to your own taste. Ultimately, you should make them your own and deliver bakes that are authentic to you!

ARE THESE RECIPES TRULY AUTHENTIC?

Why did I write this book?

My dad has never been very good at logging his recipes or baking adventures; his notes are little more than a messy collection of bare lists of ingredients, jotted down on a napkin or on an old calendar page. He has never been much of a teacher either: my direct questions on details of methods or processes were met, at most, by answers like 'you will see when it's done' or 'add enough to get the right consistency'.

It took me a couple of decades to appreciate that learning from him was not a matter of writing procedures down or listing super-accurate measurements. All I ever had to do was just be there, watching him carefully pipe that biscuit dough, coat that pastry, or decorate that cake with mesmerisingly intricate chocolate lace.

Perhaps he did not even know himself the exact ratio of flour to water he was using, but he was showing me what a 'good' pizza dough should look and feel like. And the reality is that recipes and quantities can be found in books, but no book can teach you how to smell when your sponge is done.

Only as an adult, I realised that I had unknowingly learned much more from my dad than I ever imagined and, most importantly, that through his silences and cryptic answers he had actually passed on all of his relentless passion for baking and cooking.

Those Sunday mornings spent preparing cakes for the family have built a rich collection of memories, triggered today by the same scents and flavours of those bakes. Capturing them all in a book and being able to share such a legacy far and wide fills me with pride: it is an accomplishment second to none. I can only hope that you will enjoy these bakes as much as I enjoyed writing them up. Happy baking and... *Buon Appetito!*

Some notes on the main ingredients

FLOUR

One of the most common types of flour used in Italian baking, especially when it comes to baked goods with a fine crumb, is soft wheat 00 flour. This flour has a relatively low protein content, typically below 10%, which makes it ideal for all those preparations that do not require the formation of a strong gluten network, such as sponges, pastries or biscuits. The 00 refers to the level of milling that the wheat grain has undergone, and the double zero signifies that this flour has the finest particle size on the scale.

Soft wheat 00 flour is relatively easy to find these days, being stocked by some of the largest supermarkets. It is easy to source through online retailers and specialist shops too. However, if it must be replaced, then I recommend selecting a plain (all-purpose) flour with a relatively low protein content, possibly below 10%. If using a plain flour, make sure that it is not self-raising (self-rising): no recipe in this book calls for self-raising flour as I prefer to control the type and amount of raising agent independently.

For bready bakes, I usually go for a blend of strong bread flour with a protein content around 14% (occasionally referred to as 'very strong') with others, to fine-tune the strength of the mix. A very high protein content delivers a more robust structure which can withstand longer proving slots, and it is, in cases like *babbà* (pages 67–71), indispensable. However, for most home bakes, it very often needs to be modulated, as too much gluten in the dough might turn the resulting crumb rubbery.

BUTTER

Most of the recipes in this book that call for butter will indicate whether this should be used cold, at room temperature or softened. Where there is no indication, it is because it does not matter; however, generally speaking, the initial temperature of the butter is one of the most important factors for the success of a bake. The texture of this fat changes dramatically over a relatively small range of temperatures, and the texture determines not only how well (or badly) it blends in the mixture, but also how it will interact with the other ingredients.

Cold butter should be used straight out of the fridge. Room temperature butter should have been left out of the fridge for at least 1 hour before being used. Softened butter is characterised by a creamy consistency, and it can be made in two ways: simply working room temperature butter with a spatula until it looks soft and lump-free, or starting with cold butter, dicing it, then gently microwaving it in bursts of 5 seconds until it is softened. If you use this second route, let it rest for a couple of minutes between bursts to allow all the butter to come to the same temperature. As a guide, a block of 250g (generous 1 cup) of butter softens in an 800W microwave in 15–20 seconds. When preparing softened butter it is critical not to melt it, or it will lose its creaminess entirely.

I always use unsalted butter in my bakes and, if needed, add the relevant amount of salt separately. If you use salted butter, make sure that the amount of added salt is appropriately reduced or eliminated altogether.

GIUSEPPE'S ITALIAN BAKES

LARD

Lard is no longer a fashionable ingredient: despite granting pastries with unbeatable crumbliness, its animal origin and pungent flavour do not make it a popular choice among bakers. It used to be common in many sweet and savoury bakes as a cheap and readily available fat, but today it is often replaced by other alternatives, like butter or shortening. However, my ambition is to provide you with recipes that are as close as possible to the original Italian version, therefore I am still adopting it, especially in those very traditional bakes, such as *sfogliatelle frolle* (pages 144–5) or *cannoli siciliani* (pages 148–51), where it makes a tangible difference to the end result. If lard really does not do it for you, replace it with the same amount of unsalted butter.

YEAST

Most of my savoury bakes (and a few of the sweet) call for dry yeast: this is also known as 'instant yeast' and it is the type suitable for use in bread-making machines. It does not require rehydration and it can be dropped directly in with the other ingredients. You can swap it with the same amount of 'active dry' or 'dried active' yeast, but in this case you need to rehydrate it in warm water (or milk) and sugar before adding it to the mixture. Follow the packet instructions and use part of the liquid and sugar required in the recipe to make sure that you do not alter the ratio of ingredients. You can also use fresh yeast, usually sold in foil-wrapped cubes: you can still crumble it directly in with the other ingredients, but you will need to use three times the weight of dry yeast required in the recipe.

BAKING AMMONIA

Baking ammonia, also known as baker's ammonia or ammonium carbonate, is a powerful leavening agent very common in European baking, and difficult to replace with alternative ingredients.

It is often added to dry biscuits, especially to fatless doughs, as it provides an unbeatable crispiness to the crumb.

Baking ammonia works in exactly the same way as baking soda or baking powder, i.e. by releasing gases upon heating, which inflate the dough. Some pharmacies stock baking ammonia, although it is probably just as easily sourced through online retailers, especially from Italian or German vendors, as *ammoniaca per dolci* or *Hirschhornsalz*, respectively.

Where it is impossible or impractical to source it, it can, in principle, be replaced by twice the amount of baking powder. However, the result will not be the same and the crumb will have more of a bite.

VANILLA

Very few sweet recipes in this book do not use at least a minimal amount of vanilla: this powerful flavouring adds a subtle but critical background sweetness to most bakes, and I consider it almost irreplaceable.

In the past, I have been a strenuous fan of fresh vanilla pods and firmly against the use of any liquid extract: their effectiveness varies significantly with the quality of the product, and, in some cases, the amount needed would end up altering the texture of the batter or dough.

In the last few years, I have been converted to the use of an organic vanilla bean paste instead of fresh pods and I have found it so convenient and cost effective that all the recipes in this book call for it. It is a much more concentrated version of conventional extracts, it is a completely natural product, and it includes the all-important vanilla seeds. One teaspoon of bean paste delivers roughly as much flavour as the seeds scraped off one vanilla pod.

LEMON AND ORANGE ZEST

I can think of very few Italian bakes that do not require the addition of a citrus flavour at some point: the fresh and tangy lemon fragrance is perfect to mask the eggyness of sponges or shortcrust pastries, while the sweet orange scent is the perfect companion to many other traditional flavours, such as almond, chocolate, or fresh fruit in general.

There is no decent alternative to freshly grated citrus zest, so I recommend, wherever possible, to use the zest of untreated fruits. While this is easier in Italy, where every garden, even the smallest, has its own lemon tree, it might be trickier abroad. Where untreated fruits are not available, organic, unwaxed lemons and oranges are the next best thing, and usually available in most supermarkets.

CANDIED CITRUS PEEL

As well as the zest, many bakes are flavoured with the entire peel of the citrus fruit, candied. In some cases, like in *cannoli* or *pastiera*, candied peels are a critical element of the flavour palette, and it is therefore important that they are of the best possible quality. I recommend using peels supplied in large pieces and diced as needed, as they tend to be much less sugary and retain their scent, flavour and texture much better than pre-chopped versions.

When picking the peel, there is no need to buy every fruit available: focus rather on citron and orange as the key ones. For the sake of clarity, citron is not French lemon, but a very ancient type of citrus fruit, called *cedro* in Italian.

RICOTTA

Ricotta is a very humble but extremely versatile dairy product. It is made with the whey left over from cheese production, so very often it was the only produce that farmers kept for themselves after having sold the more lucrative cheeses.

Unsurprisingly, ricotta has found its way into many rustic home bakes and it is the key ingredient in some of the most quintessentially Italian desserts, like *cannoli siciliani* (pages 148–51) or *pastiera* (pages 33–6). The original recipes call frequently for artisanal sheep's milk ricotta for its flavour, texture and pretty much perfect fat content. Despite such appealing qualities, this type of ricotta is, unfortunately, not always easy to source outside Italy, as it is very perishable, and it does not travel well. Most supermarkets, however, do sell industrial-grade, cow's milk ricotta: while not the same as the real thing, this is a reasonable alternative.

When using any ricotta, it is imperative to strain the excess liquid overnight, or for 2 days, as the watery content, however small, dissolves the sugar that is always added to ricotta-based creams, turning the resulting mixture from a thick paste into a sloppy, unmanageable mush.

GELATINE

Only a handful of recipes in this book use gelatine as a thickening agent; however, where this ingredient is needed, it is crucial that the amount is measured very accurately, as too little or too much might have disastrous effects on the texture of the final product: only a few grams of gelatine separate a silky *panna cotta* from a rubbery chewing gum!

I always use platinum-grade leaf gelatine: this is usually the strongest grade available to home bakers. Along with the weight of gelatine, I also refer to the number of leaves. If you would rather use conventional, powdered gelatine, 6.5g of platinum-grade leaf gelatine (i.e. 4 leaves) sets as much as 13g of standard powdered gelatine.

ALMONDS, HAZELNUTS AND PISTACHIOS

Traditional Italian bakes use plenty of nuts, especially almonds, hazelnuts and pistachios, mostly because of the local availability of very good quality produce at reasonable prices. Almond paste is ubiquitous all over the country but practically an essential ingredient in the southern regions, pistachios are referred to as 'green gold' in Sicily because of their prelevance in the local cuisine, while hazelnuts are almost the culinary staple of the north.

Unsurprisingly, nuts are listed as the key ingredient in many of this book's recipes and called upon in many different forms: skinned or unblanched, whole or ground. In principle, it is always best to use unprocessed nuts, simply because they retain their flavour and freshness better than those that are pre-ground or pre-chopped. Those recipes where it is critical to use whole nuts will include the processing steps to blanch, chop or grind them, whereas, when consistency is key to the success of the bake, the recipe will refer to the appropriate processed products. For those that would rather do it all from scratch, the guidelines below give indications on how to process nuts to adapt them to the recipe's needs.

Blanching. Blanching nuts allows you to loosen and remove their skin. The process is very easy and quite quick: to blanch almonds or pistachios, place them in a bowl and pour enough boiling water to cover them completely, cover the bowl with a plate or a lid and leave the nuts to soak for 3 minutes until the skin is loosened. Drain the nuts, rinse them under cold running water and remove their skin by pinching it off each kernel one by one.

Hazelnuts are slightly more stubborn and need more encouragement to let go of their skin: in this case you have to bring the water to the boil in a medium saucepan, add baking soda in a ratio of 3 tablespoons to 500ml (2 cups) water, drop the hazelnuts in and keep simmering over a low heat for 3 minutes. Follow the same steps as per almonds or pistachios to remove the skin.

Lay the blanched nuts over a baking tray in a single layer and let them dry out completely before using them or storing them.

Roasting. Roasting nuts releases their fragrance, and it gives them a unique richness, depth and complexity of flavour. In some cases, such as for *gianduia* cream (pages 210–11) or *baci di Alassio* (pages 94–7), roasting the nuts is imperative, but for other bakes, like *ricciarelli* (pages 107–8) or *paste di pistacchio* (pages 207–8), the more delicate flavour of raw nuts is more appropriate.

Roasting nuts is extremely simple, and it only requires baking them at 180°C fan (400°F/ Gas mark 6) for about 8 minutes in the case of almonds and hazelnuts, or 6 minutes in the case of pistachios. Keep a very close eye on the nuts as the step from perfectly roasted to burnt is very short! If in doubt, it is safer to take them out of the oven a minute earlier rather than later. Give the baking tray a good shake to toss them around halfway through and ensure that they are evenly roasted. If you have many nuts to roast, it is best to do it in batches. Once they are out of the oven, let them cool completely before using them.

When roasting unblanched hazelnuts, they can be skinned at the same time: wrap them in a towel and keep them warm for 10 minutes when they come out of the oven, then massage them in the towel to peel off most of the skin. Any stubborn flakes can be removed by rubbing the warm nuts between the palms of your hands.

Grinding. Nuts can be easily ground at home in any good food processor, as long as the machine is capable of delivering a powerful enough blitz to process them quickly. Low-power machines will require longer processing times, which may overheat the nuts and facilitate an undesirable release of oils. If the food processor has the option, pulsing the nuts is ideal; alternatively, they should be processed at the maximum speed just long enough to reduce them to a sandy texture.

Some notes on equipment

SCALES

If you follow a single piece of advice in this book, let it be this: buy yourself digital kitchen scales and weigh everything! If you want to nail the perfect structure, it is absolutely critical that your measurements are as accurate as possible. I rely on volumetric measurements (i.e. teaspoons or tablespoons) only for relatively small quantities, where weighing becomes too fiddly, but for everything else, including liquids, I always measure in weight. You do not need expensive scales: a set that costs the equivalent of three or four lattes will do the trick, and it will pay off with years of successful bakes!

OVEN AND MIXER

Out of the many toys in any baker's kitchen, the oven and the mixer are undoubtedly the most precious and often the most expensive. Unless there is a good reason not to, I tend to use the oven in 'static' configuration, sometimes also called 'conventional': with this setup, two heating elements, one at the top and one at the bottom of the oven chamber, heat it up to reach the set temperature. In selected cases, however, for example for pizza, it is best to select the 'fan' configuration, also called 'convection' or 'forced air', where the air is circulated in the oven chamber by a fan, allowing more items to be baked at the same time and, in theory, with a better heat distribution.

I find that the static configuration is gentler compared to fan and it provides an even heat distribution over the bake; unless stated otherwise, all the recipes in this book use the oven in static configuration. It is, however, only suitable for baking a single item at a time. If you would rather use fan, reduce the temperature given for the static configuration by 15–20°C.

The mixer is perhaps not as critical as the oven, in that, in principle, batters and doughs can be worked by hand, although whisking egg whites to stiff peaks by hand does require a very strong personal motivation... I must admit that I happily delegate the job to my electric companions; in fact all recipes in this book assume that a stand mixer or a handheld electric whisk are available, with some recipes using them both.

TOOLS

All recipes in this book are traditional home bakes, and therefore by definition do-able with very basic baking equipment. I have intentionally restricted the amount of baking tins, pastry cutters and piping nozzles to as small a selection as possible, so you should be able to bake almost everything in this book just with a decent range of standard sets. When specialist moulds are required, like for *babbà* (pages 67–71) or *pasticciotti* (pages 113–15), I have provided some indications on more common alternatives that can be used instead.

I certainly do not advocate spending a fortune on gadgets or extravagant devices, but there are a few items that can definitely make your life in the kitchen much easier. Overleaf is a list of simple tools that I cannot do without, ranked in order of decreasing importance; none is indispensable, but they will all undoubtedly contribute to the success of your bakes.

RECOMMENDED

Measuring spoons. Every single recipe in this book requires them. A set that goes down to ⅛ teaspoon is ideal. Remember to level the top with the back of a knife when measuring critical ingredients such as yeast or baking powder.

Timer. Sounds obvious, but for most bakes 2 minutes too many or too little can make it or break it. A good, reliable timer is really helpful; thankfully we all have one on our smartphones these days.

Extra-long rolling pin. When it comes to rolling pins, size does matter: a 50cm (20in) long rolling pin allows you to roll larger sheets of pastry in one go, and to transfer them over the tin easily.

Spacer rings. If you decide to buy one thing, let it be a set of spacer rings: these are gauged silicone rings that you slide on either ends of your rolling pin to make sure that you are rolling your pastry or dough to the correct thickness. I find that even just 1mm (1/32in) difference has a significant impact on the baking time and resulting texture. Check that the internal diameter of the rings matches the external diameter of your rolling pin.

Scrapers. A scraper is your best friend when you are handling wetter pastries or doughs. They are extremely cheap to buy but invaluable when you need one. All you need is a straight metal scraper and a curved plastic one.

Pasta maker. A handful of recipes in this book require rolling dough to 1–2mm (1/16in) thickness. While this is do-able by hand, it is much easier (and much more fun) with a pasta maker. Also, lamination of the dough through the progressively narrower gaps between its rollers is often a critical step to refine the texture of the dough itself, and very difficult to replicate without this machine.

Thermometer. Only a couple of common baking processes, usually involving eggs or sugar, demand the use of a cooking thermometer to monitor the temperature. Unfortunately, such processes are rather critical to some recipes and there are very few alternatives to the purchase of a digital toy. If you do buy one, invest in a tool that reads the temperature fast: the extra few seconds that a basic thermometer takes to reach an accurate reading might be enough to turn your egg mixture into scrambled eggs.

GOOD TO HAVE

Citrus zester. Lemon and orange zest typically accumulate between the protruding spikes of conventional graters: we have all had to scrape off the fragrant pulp from a grater with the tip of a knife. Dedicated zesters are specifically designed to avoid this and to shave off only the flavoursome part of the fruit skin, leaving the bitter white pith behind. After using a proper citrus zester once, you will never look back.

Flour sifter. A flour sifter will allow you to sift flour into your batter with a single hand, while the other folds it in. A sifter makes it easier to weigh the flour in advance too without having to juggle with a sieve and a bowl.

Cake slicer. Not needed if you can accurately slice three discs of equal thickness out of a single block of sponge. I certainly cannot.

Spatulas. There is no need to buy every single shape, material or size available; I only recommend three: a small offset spatula to level off batters and fillings, a long straight spatula to flatten out the tops and sides of cakes, and a silicone spatula to fold dry ingredients into whipped mixtures.

SOME NOTES ON EQUIPMENT

Cakes
& Tarts

Part 1

Torta Sette Vasetti alle Mele
Seven-Pot Cake with Apples — nut-free

SERVES UP TO 12
FOR A 24CM (9½IN), 2.5-LITRE (87-FL OZ)
BUNDT TIN

3 medium apples or 2 large
2 pots soft wheat 00 flour, plus 2 tbsp
    for dusting the apples
1 pot natural yogurt
1 pot demerara sugar
1 pot cornflour (cornstarch)
1 tsp ground cinnamon
2 tsp baking powder
3 medium eggs, at room temperature
1 pot caster (superfine) sugar
1 tsp vanilla bean paste
⅛ tsp salt
1 pot sunflower or corn oil, plus extra
    for greasing
zest of 1 organic lemon
icing (confectioners') sugar, for dusting

Torta Sette Vasetti is a modern Italian classic: the basic batter is made by measuring the ingredients by volume with a yogurt pot rather than by weight. I must admit that the engineering side of my brain struggled to accept the blanket ban on grams or centimetres in this recipe, but I cannot deny that the result is surprisingly good even without my usual pedantic control over measures and amounts…

It all starts with a single-serving yogurt pot: this recipe works equally well whether the pot is 125ml (4fl oz) or 150ml (5fl oz). Once the yogurt has been used, the pot then becomes the unit of measure for all other key ingredients.

The traditional version of this cake is a simple sponge, but I once tried adding apples to the mixture and have never looked back. Use a sweet variety like ripe Golden Delicious or Gala for best results. Despite being a relatively simple recipe, this cake can be easily elevated to a sophisticated afternoon treat by baking it in a bundt tin.

Typically, the recipe calls for natural, unsweetened yogurt, but Greek-style or flavoured ones also work rather well. The latter may add a pleasant fruity note to the sponge, but you might want to reduce the amount of sugar in the batter to balance the overall sweetness.

1. Set the shelf so that the top of the tin sits just below the middle of the oven and preheat it to 170°C (340°F/Gas mark 3). Grease and thoroughly flour the bundt tin.
2. Wash, peel and core the apples, then dice the flesh into pea-sized pieces. (Larger pieces are more likely to sink in the batter while baking.) Place the diced apples in a medium bowl and sprinkle them with 2 tablespoons of flour. Mix to coat them evenly and set aside. The flour coating will prevent the pieces of apple from sinking in the batter while baking and will slow their browning. In any case, a slight browning should be expected but it will not compromise their taste.
3. Place the yogurt in a small bowl, rinse and dry the pot and add one measure of demerara sugar to the bowl. When measuring powders with the yogurt pot, always tap it gently on the worktop to get rid any potential air pockets. Whisk until most of the sugar has dissolved in the yogurt: the mixture should look creamy and lump-free. Set aside.

CAKES & TARTS

4. Place a large sieve over a bowl and sift in both flours, the cinnamon and baking powder. Set aside.

5. Separate the eggs, placing the yolks in the bowl of a stand mixer fitted with the whisk attachment, and the whites in another medium, metal bowl. Fill the yogurt pot with caster sugar and add half to the yolks, half to the whites. Add the vanilla to the yolks and start the mixer. Whisk the mixture on high speed for about 5–6 minutes until pale and foamy.

6. Meanwhile, add the salt to the egg whites and whisk them with a handheld electric whisk for 2–3 minutes until they form glossy, stiff peaks. Set aside.

7. When the yolks are light and frothy, measure one pot of oil and trickle it slowly along the sides of the bowl while whisking. Add the yogurt and sugar mixture too and let the mixer incorporate it. Remove the bowl from the mixer, add the sifted dry ingredients, then the lemon zest and fold to combine. Add the apples and fold them in. Gently fold the whipped whites into the yolk mixture in 3 batches using a silicone spatula, then pour the resulting batter into the prepared tin. Bake for 50–52 minutes or until a skewer inserted into the deepest part of the tin comes out clean. The top of the cake should be caramel in colour and the rim should slightly come off the sides of the tin. Remove from the oven and let the cake cool in the tin.

8. When cool enough to handle, turn the cake on to a serving plate and lightly dust with icing sugar. Store under a cake dome for up to 3–4 days or freeze for up to a month.

ALSO TRY...
For a simpler version, omit the apples and for a different flavour combination swap them for 200g (7oz) fresh berries.

Torta della Nonna
Grandma's Pie

SERVES UP TO 14
FOR A 27CM (10¾IN), 4CM (1½IN) DEEP TIN

For the *pasta frolla* pastry
400g (4 cups) soft wheat 00 flour, plus extra
    for dusting
200g (scant 1 cup) cold unsalted butter, diced,
    plus extra for greasing
140g (1 cup) icing (confectioners') sugar
100g (3½oz) egg (about 2 medium eggs), cold
zest of 1 organic lemon
1 tsp vanilla bean paste
⅛ tsp salt

For the cream filling
500g (2 cups) whole milk
1 tsp vanilla bean paste
75g (2½oz) egg yolk (about 4 medium egg yolks)
110g (scant ⅔ cup) caster (superfine) sugar
40g (scant ½ cup) cornflour (cornstarch)
small pinch of salt
80g (⅓ cup) pistachio butter (pages 207–8)

For the assembly
1 egg white, for brushing
50g (⅓ cup) unsalted pistachio kernels
50g (⅓ cup) pine nut kernels
icing (confectioners') sugar, for dusting

The original version of *torta della nonna* is made with a sweet shortcrust casing filled with pastry cream and decorated with pine nuts. Its origins are in Tuscany, where it became ubiquitous in restaurants in the 80s; however, this traditional and unassuming tart has now been adopted all over the country as a classic, very simple but versatile dessert. My version is filled with pistachio cream and decorated with pistachios, but this basic recipe can be the starting point for several versions using any of the cream fillings in the Basics chapter (pages 204–11) and a matching crunchy topping.

Both filling and pastry can be prepared in advance, making this an accessible bake even for those with little time. *Torta della nonna* can be enjoyed as an end-of-meal dessert but it is particularly appreciated by kids as a mid-afternoon treat.

MAKE THE PASTRY CASING

1. Prepare the *pasta frolla* following the method on page 217. *Pasta frolla* can be prepared up to a couple of days in advance and stored wrapped in clingfilm in the fridge until needed.
2. Grease and flour the tin, including the sides. Line the bottom with a disc of baking paper.
3. Take the pastry out of the fridge, unwrap it and divide it into 2 pieces, one slightly larger than the other. Roll the larger piece to a thickness of 5mm (¼in) on a well-floured worktop, shaping it into a disc. Wrap the pastry around the rolling pin and unroll it over the prepared tin. Gently fit the pastry into the tin so that it fits snugly. Trim off the excess pastry by running a blunt knife along the rim of the tin. Set aside.
4. Now prepare the pastry top: roll the smaller piece of pastry to a thickness of 5mm (¼in) and shape it into a disc. Leave on the worktop for later.

MAKE THE CREAM FILLING

5. Prepare one batch of pistachio cream following the method on pages 207–8. The cream filling should be prepared at least 1–2 hours before it is needed to give it time to cool to room temperature. The pastry should never be filled with warm cream.

ASSEMBLE

6. Place the shelf in the lowest position in the oven and preheat it to 180°C (350°F/ Gas mark 4).
7. Prick the pastry base in several places with a fork, spoon in the cream filling and level it with an offset spatula or a spoon.
8. Wrap the pastry top around the rolling pin and unroll it over the filling. Pinch it to the pastry base around the sides of the tin to seal the two together, then trim off the excess pastry by running a blunt knife along the rim. Fold the pastry on the sides of the tin inwards, towards the centre of the tart, and create slits in the pastry rim with the back of a knife. Brush the pastry with egg white and prick a few holes in it using a fork or a cocktail stick.
9. Roughly chop the pistachio kernels and sprinkle them over the top of the pie. Sprinkle over the pine nut kernels too. Bake in the oven immediately for 45 minutes. The pie is ready when the pastry top is a light caramel colour and just starting to swell. Let the pie cool completely before removing from the tin.
10. Decorate with a light dusting of icing sugar when cold. Store in the fridge for up to 2–3 days.

ALSO TRY…

For the traditional combination, use basic pastry cream (pages 204–6) with pine nut kernels for decoration. And for additional tanginess, dot the filling with a handful of Amarena cherries in syrup.

Chocolate lovers might prefer what is known as *torta del nonno* (grandpa's pie), made with chocolate cream filling (page 206) and topped with flaked almonds. My personal favourite, however, is a coffee and sambuca cream (page 206) with pecan topping.

Amor Polenta
Polenta Sponge Cake

SERVES UP TO 10
FOR A 30 X 12CM (12 X 4½IN) HALF-ROUND TIN
OR LOAF TIN

For the sponge
150g (5½oz) egg (about 3 medium eggs),
    at room temperature
120g (¾ cup) caster (superfine) sugar
1 tsp vanilla bean paste
100g (scant ½ cup) unsalted butter, plus
    extra for greasing
zest of 1 organic lemon
zest of 1 organic orange
½ tsp natural almond extract
2 tbsp amaretto liqueur (or rum)
70g (¾ cup) soft wheat 00 flour, plus extra
    for dusting
1 tsp baking powder
⅛ tsp salt
60g (⅓ cup) finely ground cornmeal (polenta)
100g (1 cup) ground almonds
icing (confectioners') sugar, for dusting

For the decoration (optional)
10-12 fresh raspberries
100g (scant ½ cup) whipping cream
    (35–40% fat), cold
20g (generous 1 tbsp) icing (confectioners') sugar
½ tsp vanilla bean paste

Amor polenta is traditionally baked in a half-round, ribbed loaf tin; but any loaf tin will do. It is quick to make, as all the ingredients are worked in the mixer bowl, nevertheless, the result is a moist and light sponge, rustic and with a little bite. The batter only includes a minimal amount of leavening agent; most of the spongy structure is the result of the vigorous whipping of the eggs, so do not cut this step short.

MAKE THE SPONGE

1. Grease the tin well and dust it with flour. Place the shelf in the middle of the oven and preheat it to 170°C (340°F/Gas mark 3).
2. Add the eggs, sugar and vanilla to the bowl of a stand mixer fitted with the whisk attachment and whip the mixture for 6–8 minutes on high speed until it triples in volume and looks pale and frothy. Meanwhile, melt the butter in a small microwave-safe bowl: 40 seconds in a 800W microwave should be enough. Set aside to cool. When the egg mixture is light and fluffy, add the citrus zests, almond extract and liqueur, and gently whisk to incorporate them.
3. Sift the flour, baking powder and salt into the mixture, add the cornmeal and ground almonds, and fold them in with a silicone spatula until fully combined. Finally, fold in the melted butter. Ensure that the butter is fully incorporated by scraping the sides of the bowl thoroughly with the spatula. Pour the batter into the prepared tin and bake for 28–30 minutes, or until the top of the cake is caramel in colour and a skewer inserted into the deepest part of the tin comes out clean. Let the cake cool completely in the tin and then turn it on to a serving plate. Coat the top of the cake with a light dusting of icing sugar.

DECORATE

4. Prepare the Chantilly cream following the method on page 75 and place it in a piping bag with a 12mm (½in) star nozzle. Pipe dollops of cream along the sponge and place a raspberry on each one. Store under a cake dome for up to 3–4 days or freeze for up to a month.

Torta Tenerina
Little Tender Cake

— nut-free

SERVES UP TO 12
FOR A 23CM (9IN) SPRINGFORM CAKE TIN

200g (7oz) dark chocolate chips or bar, broken
    into small pieces (70–75% cocoa solids)
125g (generous ½ cup) unsalted butter, diced,
    plus extra for greasing
150g (5½oz) egg (about 3 medium eggs),
    at room temperature, separated
pinch of salt
140g (¾ cup) caster (superfine) sugar
50g (½ cup) soft wheat 00 flour, plus extra
    for dusting
3 tbsp whole milk
unsweetened cocoa powder, for dusting
icing (confectioners') sugar, for dusting
3 chocolate truffles, to decorate (optional)

Tenerina means 'small and tender' and it is
a very good description of the texture of this
cake. It does not call for any raising agent, so
the result is a shallow, dense but moist, very
chocolatey cake.

It originates from Ferrara, in Emilia
Romagna, where it is also known as *tacolenta*
(sticky) because of its peculiar, almost creamy
core. The key to a good *tenerina* is the baking
time: too long and it will dry out, too short and
it might retain a raw core. I test the bake by
monitoring the skin: as soon as this turns dull
and crispy, the cake is done.

A springform tin is ideal for baking a
tenerina as the structure is too delicate to
turn out of a standard tin. The texture is very
rich and exclusively for chocolate lovers, but
everybody will love it with whipped cream or
vanilla ice cream. I like to decorate the top with
chocolate truffles, but this is entirely optional.

1. Set the shelf in the middle of the oven
and preheat it to 180°C (350°F/Gas mark
4). Grease the tin and line the bottom with
baking paper.
2. Melt the chocolate and butter in a metal bowl
over gently simmering water, ensuring that the
bottom of the bowl does not touch the water.
Stir with a silicone spatula until homogeneous
and set aside to cool.
3. Beat the egg whites with the salt using
a handheld electric whisk until foamy.
Gradually add half of the sugar and keep
beating to make a stiff meringue. Do not over-
beat the whites or it will be more difficult
to incorporate them into the batter: the
meringue should form stiff, shiny peaks but
not look dry and clumpy. Set the meringue
aside and, in another bowl, use the whisk
to beat the egg yolks with the remaining 70g
(⅓ cup) sugar until pale and fluffy.
4. Sift the flour into the yolk and sugar mixture
and keep whisking at minimum speed until
smooth. Pour in the chocolate and butter,
then add the milk and whisk again until fully
combined. Gently fold the meringue into the
chocolate batter in 3 stages with a silicone
spatula. Pour into the prepared tin and bake
for 20–22 minutes until the skin looks dull
and crispy.
5. Leave to cool in the tin for 10 minutes, then
remove the ring and transfer the cake to a
cooling rack to cool completely. Once cool,
dust it with cocoa powder, then coat two
thirds of the top with a generous layer of
icing sugar. Place the truffles (if using) across
the boundary between the cocoa and sugar.
Store under a cake dome for up to 3–4 days.

Torta Paradiso
Paradise Cake

— nut-free

SERVES UP TO 12
FOR A 23CM (9IN) SPRINGFORM CAKE TIN

For the sponge
250g (1 cup plus 2 tbsp) unsalted butter,
    softened (see page 9), plus extra
    for greasing
250g (1⅔ cups) caster (superfine) sugar
1 tsp vanilla bean paste
zest of 1 organic unwaxed lemon
250g (9oz) egg (about 5 medium eggs),
    at room temperature
125g (1¼ cups) soft wheat 00 flour
125g (1¼ cups) cornflour (cornstarch)
1½ tsp baking powder
pinch of salt
icing (confectioners') sugar, for dusting

For the milk cream
350g (1½ cups) whole milk
1 tbsp clear honey
70g (⅓ cup) caster (superfine) sugar
1 tsp vanilla bean paste
40g (scant ½ cup) cornflour (cornstarch)
150g (⅔ cup) whipping (heavy) cream
    (at least 30% fat)

A bakery in Pavia claims to have invented the Paradise Cake in the 19th century and still holds the secret to the original recipe. The name refers to the heavenly, almost cloud-like crumb which is the fingerprint of this sponge. There are some debates around the presence of a raising agent in the original ingredients list; in this recipe, and in most of the versions commonly adopted today, a minimal amount of baking powder is included just to ensure

success; however, incorporating air into the batter through energetic whipping is still crucial to achieve the coveted paradisiac structure.

Traditionally, it is served without a filling, and it is delicious as it is, but I prefer it filled with a thick and generous layer of a delicate *crema al latte* (milk cream). This combination has become very popular in Italy since the early 90s, when Ferrero started to market a very successful version of Paradise Cake.

MAKE THE SPONGE

1. Set the shelf in the lowest part of the oven and preheat it to 180°C (350°F/Gas mark 4). Grease the tin and line the bottom with a disc of baking paper.

2. Transfer the butter to the bowl of a stand mixer fitted with the whisk attachment. Add the sugar, vanilla and lemon zest and whisk for 7–8 minutes until the mixture is soft and creamy. Start at very low speed and gradually increase to full speed as the butter softens.

3. Weigh the eggs in a spouted jug and incorporate them one at a time, waiting until the previous egg is fully incorporated in the batter before adding the next. Scrape the sides of the bowl as needed and once all the eggs have been added, keep beating on high speed for a further 7–8 minutes until pale and fluffy. Do not be tempted to rush this step as it is critical to incorporate as much air as possible into the batter to ensure the cake is very soft.

4. At this point the batter might look slightly curdled, but this is to be expected. Sift the flour, cornflour, baking powder and salt

together and gently fold it into the egg mixture in 3 batches. Use very delicate movements to avoid knocking the air out. Pour the batter into the prepared tin and bake for 45 minutes or until a skewer inserted into the centre of the cake comes out clean and dry.

5. Leave to cool in the tin for 10 minutes, then remove the ring and transfer the cake to a cooling rack to cool completely.

MAKE THE MILK CREAM

6. Pour about 300g (1¼ cups + 1 tbsp) of the milk into a small pan, add the honey, sugar and vanilla and gently bring to a simmer over a low heat.

7. Sift the cornflour into the remaining 50g (scant ¼ cup) cold milk and stir it well with a whisk until all the flour is dissolved and no clumps are visible. Pour the cold milk into the hot milk pan and bring it back to a simmer over a very low heat until the mixture falls back from the whisk in thick ribbons. This will take a couple of minutes.

8. Pour the mixture into a bowl, line the surface with clingfilm and let cool to room temperature, then chill in the fridge until set.

9. Meanwhile, whip the cream to stiff peaks – it will take about 2–3 minutes. Once the surface is completely dull and no longer shiny, the cream is ready.

10. Once the milk mixture is completely cold, take it out of the fridge and whisk it again with a handheld electric whisk until creamy. Gently fold the whipped cream into the milk mixture in 3 stages.

ASSEMBLE

11. Slice the sponge horizontally to divide it into 2 equal discs. Secure the bottom disc of sponge to the serving plate with a small dollop of cream.

12. Spread the cream over the bottom disc of sponge and level it out with a spatula or a spoon. Place the remaining disc of sponge over the cream and press it down gently until the cream starts bulging from the sides of the cake. Using a spatula or a cake scraper, remove the excess cream from around the sides of the sponge.

13. Dust the cake lightly with icing sugar. Store in the fridge for up to 2 days.

ALSO TRY...

The paradise sponge is an ideal base for a delicate birthday cake when filled with *crema pasticcera* (pages 204–6), *crema al gianduia* (pages 210–11) or even *crema al pistacchio* (pages 207–8). If you are feeling very indulgent, however, you will never go wrong by simply packing it with a good layer of chocolate and hazelnut spread.

Pastiera

— nut-free

SERVES UP TO 14
FOR A 27CM (10¾IN), 4CM (1½IN) DEEP TIN

For the *pasta frolla* pastry

400g (4 cups) soft wheat 00 flour, plus extra
  for dusting
200g (scant 1 cup) unsalted butter, cold
140g (1 cup) icing (confectioners') sugar
100g (3½oz) egg (about 2 medium eggs), cold
zest of 1 organic lemon
1 tsp vanilla bean paste
⅛ tsp salt

For the filling

300g (1⅓ cups) ricotta
200g (scant 1½ cups) cooked wheat grain
  (shop-bought or homemade, see
  page 219)
150g (scant ⅔ cup) whole milk
20g (scant 2 tbsp) unsalted butter, plus
  extra for greasing
zest of 1 organic lemon
zest of 1 organic orange
40g (⅓ cup) candied citron peel
40g (⅓ cup) candied orange peel
2 medium eggs, plus 1 medium egg yolk
240g (1⅓ cups) caster (superfine) sugar
¼ tsp ground cinnamon
1 tsp vanilla bean paste
1 tbsp natural orange blossom water
icing (confectioners') sugar, for dusting

In Campania and surrounding areas, *pastiera* is nothing less than an institution, and it is easy to understand why; I could not imagine Easter without it. For me, the sweet fragrance of orange blossom is to Easter what mulled wine and gingerbread are to Christmas: an essential part of the celebration.

The texture of *pastiera* is unique: it is not a sponge, not a cream, nor a mousse. It has a moreish, rich and phenomenally fragrant filling, dense but with a very light bite, packed with flavours but not overly sweet. If this was not enough, it is also surprisingly easy to make. The casing is simple *pasta frolla*, and the filling can be whipped up in a few minutes, providing that you have the right ingredients handy.

Sourcing them is undeniably the longest step in the process, especially outside Italy. Ideally, sieved artisanal ricotta should be used, but this is difficult to find. I use ricotta from the supermarket, and it works very well; in fact, its grain is usually already fine enough and does not need any further sieving. Two other key ingredients might take some googling, but hopefully no more than an online purchase: candied citrus peels and cooked wheat grain. The latter is essential to *pastiera* and difficult to replace. In the past I have tested rice or barley as a substitute, but nothing works as well as wheat grain. The easiest option, and what most Italians do these days, is to buy it ready-cooked: it is available in cans and jars from online retailers all over the world. However, if raw wheat grain is easier to source, cooking it is not difficult; it just takes some patience and time. The method is on page 219.

Good-quality candied citrus peels are also critical: *pastiera* is all about the fragrance and the scent, which is difficult to achieve without a good serving of high-quality citron and orange peels. The latter is easy to find in most supermarkets, citron is slightly trickier, but available online. For the sake of clarity, citron is not French lemon, but a very ancient type of citrus fruit, called *cedro* in Italian.

One final word about the orange blossom: flavourings, especially made for *pastiera*, are available from most online shops, either artificial or natural: those sold in small 2ml vials are very powerful and must be used sparingly. A single vial is more than enough for one *pastiera*. However, I prefer to use larger amounts of natural orange blossom water as it does not leave any bitter aftertaste, it is 100% natural, and it has a much more delicate scent.

One ingredient not mentioned in the list is patience: *pastiera* is best eaten at least 12 hours after baking, as this will allow time for the flavours to fully develop and the moisture in the filling to soften the pastry casing. *Pastiera* is not a bake for the hasty!

1. Place the ricotta in a sieve over a bowl for at least 30 minutes to drain off any liquid. The longer you drain the ricotta, the better: if possible, drain it in the fridge overnight.

MAKE THE PASTRY CASING

2. Prepare the *pasta frolla* following the method on page 217. *Pasta frolla* can be prepared up to a couple of days in advance and stored wrapped in clingfilm in the fridge until needed.
3. Grease the tin well and dust it with flour, including the sides. Line the bottom with a disc of baking paper.
4. Take the pastry out of the fridge, unwrap it and divide it into 2 pieces, one slightly larger than the other. Roll the larger piece to a thickness of 5mm (¼in) on a well-floured worktop, shaping it into a disc. Wrap the pastry around the rolling pin and unroll it over the prepared tin. Gently fit the pastry into the tin so that it fits snugly. Trim off the excess pastry by running a blunt knife along the rim of the tin. Prick the pastry base in several places with a fork and set aside.
5. Prepare the pastry strips to decorate the top: roll the remaining pastry to a thickness of 5mm (¼in), and shape it roughly into a rectangle. Cut it into 2cm (¾in) wide strips along the long side of the rectangle. A rigid ruler and a pizza cutter are ideal here. If you use a knife, cut with a guillotine motion; avoid dragging the blade across the pastry as this will deform it.

MAKE THE FILLING

6. Place the cooked wheat grain in a saucepan and add the milk, butter and citrus zests. Bring to a simmer over a very low heat and cook, stirring continuously, until most of the liquid has evaporated and the mixture is thick and creamy. Set aside to cool to room temperature.
7. Meanwhile, dice the candied citron and orange peel so that each piece is no larger than 4–5mm (¼in).
8. Place the drained ricotta in a large bowl and add the eggs, yolk, sugar and cinnamon. Beat the mixture with a handheld electric whisk until very well combined. Add the vanilla and orange blossom water and keep beating until incorporated. Add the wheat grain mixture and the candied peels to the ricotta cream and mix until fully combined.

ASSEMBLE

9. Place the shelf in the lowest position in the oven and preheat it to 180°C (350°F/Gas mark 4).

10. Pour the filling into the pastry casing. Lay the longest pastry strip over the filling across the middle of the tin and attach it to the pastry casing at both ends, pinching off the excess lengths with your fingers. Lay 2 more pastry strips on either side of the first so that they are roughly evenly spaced across the top of the *pastiera*.

11. Lay a second set of strips, at a 45° angle to the first set to create a diamond pattern. The edges of the pastry casing should sit 5mm (¼in) above the surface of the filling; if necessary, trim off any excess pastry by running a sharp knife around the edges of the casing against the sides of the tin.

12. Bake in the oven immediately for 55 minutes– 1 hour. The *pastiera* is ready when the filling is a deep caramel colour and some small cracks are starting to appear on its surface. While baking, the filling will swell as some of the moisture turns into steam: this is to be expected and the *pastiera* will settle back almost to its original height upon cooling.

13. Let the *pastiera* cool completely before taking it out of the tin.

14. Decorate with a light dusting of icing sugar just before serving. Store in the fridge for up to a week or freeze for up to a month.

Torta Latte Caldo e Caffè
Hot Milk and Coffee Sponge Cake

— nut-free

SERVES UP TO 12
FOR A 23CM (9IN) SPRINGFORM CAKE TIN

200g (7oz) egg (about 4 medium eggs),
    at room temperature
200g (generous 1 cup) caster (superfine) sugar
100g (scant ½ cup) whole milk
80g (⅓ cup) unsalted butter, plus extra
    for greasing
80g (⅓ cup) strong espresso
220g (2¼ cups) soft wheat 00 flour
3 tsp baking powder
pinch of salt

For the cream filling
500g (2 cups) whole milk
1 tsp vanilla bean paste
75g (2½oz) egg yolk (about 5 medium
    egg yolks)
110g (scant ⅔ cup) caster (superfine) sugar
50g (½ cup) cornflour (cornstarch)
small pinch of salt
2 tbsp instant coffee

For the glaze
50g (⅓ cup) icing (confectioners') sugar
2-3 tsp strong espresso

The simplest version of hot milk cake is flavoured only with vanilla; however, I am undeniably partial to my coffee variant as the overall flavour is pleasantly close to caffè latte, the quintessential Italian (and my favourite) breakfast drink.

The sponge on its own is easy to make and is the perfect companion to a cup of coffee. However, I have filled mine with a good layer of coffee cream and drizzled it with coffee glaze to boost the flavour further. Which version you go for is entirely up to you: they both taste delicious!

MAKE THE SPONGE

1. Set the shelf in the lowest position in the oven and preheat it to 180°C (350°F/Gas mark 4). Grease the tin and line the bottom with a disc of baking paper.
2. Beat the eggs with the sugar in the bowl of a stand mixer fitted with the whisk attachment until pale and frothy. The egg mixture should reach the 'ribbon stage', i.e. the mixture should fall from the whisks in continuous ribbons, leaving a trail on the surface of the batter that does not disappear. This will take 10–15 minutes with the mixer at high speed.
3. Meanwhile, warm the milk and butter in a small pan over low heat until just simmering. Remove from the heat and incorporate the coffee.
4. Sift the flour, baking powder and salt into a bowl and gently fold it into the egg mixture in 3 stages, using a silicone spatula. Put 3 large tablespoons of the mixture in a bowl, then add the milk and coffee mixture and whisk to combine. Slowly pour this mixture into the rest of the batter, folding it in delicately with the spatula until fully combined.
5. Pour the batter into the tin and bake for 45 minutes or until a skewer inserted into the centre of the cake comes out clean and dry.
6. Leave to cool in the tin for 10 minutes, then remove the ring and transfer the cake to a cooling rack to cool completely.

MAKE THE FILLING

7. Prepare the coffee cream following the method on page 206. The filling should be prepared at least 1–2 hours before it is needed to give it time to cool to room temperature.

MAKE THE GLAZE

8. While the cake cools, prepare a simple coffee glaze by mixing the icing sugar with 2 teaspoons of espresso. This sugar-to-coffee ratio will give you a rather thick glaze, suitable for piping. If you are drizzling it with a spoon, you might need to add a third teaspoon of espresso to achieve a thinner texture. Line the surface of the glaze with clingfilm and set it aside for later.

ASSEMBLE

9. Once the sponge has cooled completely, slice it in half horizontally to divide it into 2 discs of about equal thickness.
10. Secure the bottom disc of sponge to a serving plate with a small dollop of cream. Spread the coffee cream over the bottom disc of sponge and level it out with a spatula or a spoon. Top with the remaining disc of sponge and press it down gently.
11. Drizzle the coffee glaze over the cake with a spoon or with a small piping bag fitted with a 2mm (1/16in) diameter nozzle. Store in the fridge for up to 2–3 days.

Torta co' Bischeri

SERVES UP TO 14
FOR A 27CM (10¾IN) SPRINGFORM CAKE TIN

For the *pasta frolla* pastry
400g (4 cups) soft wheat 00 flour, plus extra
    for dusting
200g (scant 1 cup) unsalted butter, cold,
    plus extra for greasing
140g (1 cup) icing (confectioners') sugar
100g (3½oz) egg (about 2 medium eggs), cold
zest of 1 organic lemon
1 tsp vanilla bean paste
⅛ tsp salt

For the filling
60g (scant ½ cup) sultanas (golden raisins)
70g (⅓ cup) vin santo (or maraschino,
    rum or Strega)
60g (2¼oz) dark chocolate chips or bar
    (50–55% cocoa solids)
40g (⅓ cup) candied citron peel or mixed
    citrus peel
700g (3 cups) whole milk
1 tsp vanilla bean paste
¼ tsp grated nutmeg
½ tsp ground cinnamon
⅛ tsp salt
100g (½ cup) short-grain pudding rice
40g (scant ½ cup) unsweetened
    cocoa powder
90g (½ cup) caster (superfine) sugar
40g (⅓ cup) pine nut kernels
100g (3½oz) egg (about 2 medium eggs), beaten

Torta co' bischeri is a sweet pie made with a crumbly *pasta frolla* casing holding a fragrant and rich chocolatey filling. It is a rustic and homely pie, originally from Pontasserchio, near Pisa, these days often served in restaurants and bars as it keeps very well, and it is conveniently served cold. The name includes a cheeky phallic reference, meaning literally 'pie with willies', because of the pointy shapes moulded all around the pastry edge.

The texture is rich and dense, but the sultanas soaked in liqueur keep it nicely moist and light. Despite the high chocolate content, it is not overly sweet as most of the flavour comes from the perfectly balanced palette of spices and candied citrus peels.

The dark top lends itself to being decorated: you can swap the traditional diamond pattern for a variety of shapes, numbers or messages cut out of the leftover pastry. In this case, place the pie in the fridge for 20 minutes before baking as this will stop the decorative pastry from melting and losing sharpness in the oven.

MAKE THE PASTRY

1. Prepare the *pasta frolla* following the method on page 217. *Pasta frolla* can be prepared up to a couple of days in advance and stored wrapped in clingfilm in the fridge until needed.

MAKE THE FILLING

2. Soak the sultanas in a small bowl with the vin santo. Stir them occasionally. If you are using a chocolate bar, roughly chop it into small pieces. Dice the citron peel so that each piece is no larger than 4–5mm (¼in).
3. Place the milk in a medium pan and add the vanilla, nutmeg, cinnamon and salt, then bring

it to a simmer over a low-medium heat. Stir the milk often to avoid it sticking to the bottom of the pan and keep a close eye on it when it starts simmering as it may boil and overspill. When the milk just starts to simmer, reduce the heat and add the rice. Let it simmer until the milk has been fully absorbed; it will take 25–30 minutes. The resulting mixture will look thick and creamy. Stir the rice often while it cooks, and continuously when the mixture starts thickening up as it might stick to the pan and burn easily otherwise.

4. Remove from the heat and sift in the cocoa powder, then add the sugar, pine nut kernels, sultanas and the vin santo, candied peels and chocolate chips. Mix while the mixture is still hot to melt the chocolate. Once fully combined, add the eggs and mix until completely incorporated. Line the surface with clingfilm and set aside to cool to room temperature, then chill in the fridge for at least 1 hour.

ASSEMBLE

5. Grease the tin well, including the sides, and line the bottom with baking paper. Place the shelf in the lowest position in the oven and preheat it to 180°C (350°F/Gas mark 4).

6. Take the pastry out of the fridge, unwrap it and roll it to a thickness of 5mm (¼in) on a well-floured worktop, shaping it into a disc. Wrap the pastry around the rolling pin and unroll it over the prepared tin. Gently fit the pastry into the tin so that it fits snugly. Let the excess pastry hang out of the tin sides without trimming it: this helps to hold the sides of the pastry casing up while you fill and shape

it. Prick the bottom of the pastry in several places with a fork.

7. Spoon the filling into the pastry casing and level it off with the back of a spoon or, better, with a small offset spatula. Trim off the excess pastry by running a blunt knife along the rim.

8. Now shape the ring of pastry above the filling to form *bischeri* around the pie. Starting from the side of the pie closest to you, use a sharp knife to cut a slit in the pastry ring: cut from the bottom of the pastry (i.e. level with the top of the filling) upwards, at a 45° angle. Fold the small flap of pastry generated by the cut in on itself, so that the cut edge now lays flush with the filling top. This will have formed a pointed shape of pastry, twice the thickness of the rest of the pastry: your first *bischero*. Progress by cutting and folding the pastry all around the pie to shape the full ring of *bischeri*.

9. To make the decorative strips for the top, briefly knead the pastry offcuts into a thick sausage and roll it to a thickness of 5mm (¼in), shaping it into a narrow sheet, 30cm (12in) long. Using a crimped pastry wheel, cut 2cm (¾in) wide strips off the pastry sheet and arrange them over the top of the pie in a geometric diamond pattern.

10. Bake for 53–55 minutes, or until the *bischeri* start to brown. While baking, the filling will swell as some of the moisture turns into steam: this is to be expected and the pie will settle back almost to its original height upon cooling. Let the pie cool completely before taking it out of the tin. Store under a cake dome for up to 3–4 days.

Bonèt

— gluten-free

SERVES UP TO 10
FOR A 30CM (12IN) LOAF TIN

For the caramel
120g (²⁄₃ cup) caster (superfine) sugar

For the batter
100g (3½oz) amaretti biscuits (shop-bought
    or homemade, see pages 88—90), plus
    a few extra to decorate
170g (5¾oz) egg yolk (about 10 medium
    egg yolks)
90g (½ cup) caster (superfine) sugar
700g (3 cups) whole milk
50g (½ cup) unsweetened cocoa powder
50g (generous 3 tbsp) amaretto liqueur
    (or coffee)
1 tsp vanilla bean paste
⅛ tsp salt

Bonèt is an ancient, flan-type dessert named, according to 19th century literature, after the shape of the pan used to bake it in, resembling a hat, or bonèt in the local dialect. The origins of bonèt are deeply rooted in Piedmont, where it is still a traditional end-of-meal dessert, typical of the Langhe region.

Preparation is simple, however, like most crème-caramel-type desserts, bonèt is baked in a bain-marie (water bath), so you will need a large roasting tray, filled with water, in which to accommodate the baking tin. The texture is similar to crème caramel, albeit with slightly more body, due to the biscuits in the batter. The flavour, however, is more robust: bonèt tastes unmistakably of amaretti and the chocolate and liqueur contribute to its bold flavour.

For bonèt, you can use shop-bought amaretti, or make your own with my recipe (see pages 88—90). Traditionally, the liqueur added to the batter was Fernet, a quintessentially Italian end-of-meal drink, but amaretto liqueur is much easier to source, and it goes very well with the almond flavour. Rum or cognac are also common alternatives, and a non-alcoholic version can be baked using the same amount of strong espresso instead.

Bonèt needs to cool and rest for at least a couple of hours in the fridge before being demoulded, to make sure that it builds its consistency fully. It is the perfect dessert to prepare in advance as it benefits from a whole night in the fridge. Amaretti biscuits are the unmissable decoration, but also a few swirls of sweet whipped cream would go very well with the dense chocolatey texture. Bonèt must be served cold.

MAKE THE CARAMEL

1. Place the loaf tin on a flat, heat-resistant surface (a wooden chopping board is ideal).
2. To make the caramel, place a metal pan with the sugar over the lowest heat on your hob and wait for the edges to start melting. At that point, occasionally tilt and shake the pan to melt all the sugar. At no point in the process should you stir the caramel. The caramel is ready as soon as all the sugar is liquid and deep amber in colour. Carefully pour the caramel into the loaf tin and swirl it around to coat the bottom. Leave on the heat-resistant surface to cool.

MAKE THE BATTER

3. Place the shelf in the middle of the oven and preheat it to 180°C (350°F/Gas mark 4).
4. Place the amaretti in the bowl of a food processor and blitz them at full speed until they turn into a fine, flour-like powder. Set aside. Place the egg yolks and the sugar in the bowl of a stand mixer fitted with the whisk attachment and whisk them at full speed for 2–3 minutes until pale and fluffy.
5. Meanwhile, place the milk in a spouted, stout, microwave-safe jug and microwave it until it is warm to the touch. Two minutes in a conventional 800W oven should be enough.
6. When the egg mixture is pale and fluffy, stop the mixer and sift in the cocoa powder, then add the liqueur, vanilla, salt and ground amaretti. Start the mixer at very low speed to combine the ingredients. Finally, add the milk and whisk again until smooth.
7. Place the loaf tin into the larger roasting tray and pour the batter into the tin. Place the baking tray and tin in the oven and carefully pour boiling water into the tray up to about three quarters of the height of the tin. Bake for 43–45 minutes. At this stage, the surface of the *bonèt* will look almost spongy and fully baked, with the edges nearly coming off the sides of the tin. The centre will still have a gentle wobble and the batter will feel quite jelly-like. Do not be tempted to wait for the *bonèt* to look completely set or it will over-bake, resulting in a tough, rubbery texture. Remove the loaf tin from the bain-marie and let it cool to room temperature, then leave it to rest in the fridge for at least a couple of hours, ideally overnight.

ASSEMBLE

8. When you are ready to serve, run a blunt knife around the sides of the baking tin, cover it with an upside-down serving plate and turn both over. Tap the plate over a folded dish towel to help the *bonèt* come out of the tin. The *bonèt* should slide out easily, but if it refuses to, dip the tin into a hot water bath for a few seconds, then repeat the previous step.
9. Decorate the top of the *bonèt* with a few amaretti biscuits and a few swirls of sweet whipped cream, if you like. Store in the fridge for up to 2–3 days.

ALSO TRY…

You will be left with a sizeable amount of egg white after baking a *bonèt*, which could be an excellent excuse to make some *ricciarelli* (pages 107–8), *brutti ma buoni* (page 116), *amaretti* (pages 88–90), *baci di Alassio* (pages 94–7) or *paste di pistacchio* (page 98). Or, if you are eager to use them all in one go, you can just bake another cake and make a *Torta Mimì* (pages 50–2). If the thought of more cake does not fill you with joy, you can swap the 170g (5¾oz) of egg yolk for 200g (7oz) of whole egg instead and use about 4 medium whole eggs for the *bonèt* batter. The resulting texture will be slightly stiffer and not as silky as with yolks only, but the flavour will still be delicious.

CAKES & TARTS

Crostata Semola e Cioccolata
Semolina and Chocolate Tart — nut-free

SERVES UP TO 14
FOR A 27CM (10¾IN) TART TIN

For the pastry
300g (3 cups) soft wheat 00 flour
150g (⅔ cup) unsalted butter, cold
100g (¾ cup) icing (confectioners') sugar
70g (2½oz) egg (about 1 medium egg and
    1 yolk), cold
zest of 1 organic lemon
1 tsp vanilla bean paste
pinch of salt

For the filling
400g (1¾ cups) ricotta
120g (⅔ cup) caster (superfine) sugar
1 tsp vanilla bean paste
500g (2 cups) whole milk
½ tsp ground cinnamon
100g (⅔ cup) semolina
30g (2 tbsp) unsalted butter
zest of 1 organic orange
50g (generous 3 tbsp) vin santo (optional)

For the ganache
120g (4¼oz) dark chocolate chips or bar
    (50–55% cocoa solids)
160g (¾ cup) double (heavy) cream
    (48–50% fat)
25g (scant 2 tbsp) unsalted butter

To decorate
250g (9oz) mixed fresh fruit, such as
    strawberries, cherries, kiwis, grapes
    or mixed berries

The semolina and chocolate tart is a traditional and rustic dessert from Tuscany, in the past baked to celebrate Easter, but these days available throughout the region all year round. Do not be fooled by the list of humble and old-fashioned ingredients: this tart truly elevates semolina and ricotta to the status of the most sophisticated dessert. The crumbly *pasta frolla* casing holds a soft cream filling, flavoured with orange, cinnamon and, at times, vin santo. This unassuming layer of semolina cream is then topped by the most decadent and rich chocolate ganache: the combination is perfectly balanced, not overly sweet and extremely satisfying.

The traditional version of this tart does not include any decoration, but I have always loved crowning it with a generous helping of fresh fruit, partially because the contrast of the colourful array with the dark background looks simply stunning, but also because the tanginess of the fruit goes very well with the sweetness of the ganache and the creaminess of the filling.

To retain the silky texture of the chocolate and the softness of the semolina cream, it is best to serve this tart at room temperature.

1. The day before baking, place the ricotta in a sieve over a bowl and keep it in the fridge overnight to drain off any excess liquid. This step is really important to avoid an overly wet filling which would soak the pastry casing and deliver a dreaded soggy bottom.

MAKE THE PASTRY

2. Prepare the *pasta frolla* following the method on page 217. *Pasta frolla* can be prepared up to a couple of days in advance and stored wrapped in clingfilm in the fridge until needed.

MAKE THE FILLING

3. Once drained, shop-bought ricotta can be used as it is, artisanal ricotta will need sieving. This can be done by pushing it through the mesh of a strainer with the back of a spoon. Place the ricotta in a medium bowl and whisk it with a handheld electric whisk until creamy. Add the sugar and vanilla and whisk again to combine. Set aside.

4. Weigh the milk in a medium pan, add the cinnamon and bring to a simmer over a medium heat. The pan must be large enough to also fit the ricotta and sugar mixture later. When the milk starts simmering, reduce the heat and add the semolina gradually, sprinkling it in a little at a time from above, while vigorously and continuously stirring the milk with a whisk: this will avoid the formation of lumps. When the mixture becomes too stiff for the whisk, mix it with a wooden spoon and keep stirring over a low heat for 3–4 minutes to produce a thick cream. Take the semolina off the heat and, while it is still hot, add the butter. Stir to melt and incorporate it. While the semolina is still warm, add the ricotta mixture in 3 batches, incorporating each one fully before adding the next. Add the orange zest and the vin santo (if using), combine and set aside to cool.

MAKE THE CASING AND BAKE

5. While the filling cools, grease and flour the tin well, including the sides. Line the bottom with baking paper.

6. Take the pastry out of the fridge, unwrap it and roll it to a thickness of 5mm (¼in) over a well-floured worktop, shaping it as a disc. Wrap the pastry around the rolling pin and unroll it over the prepared tin. Gently fit the pastry into the tin so that it fits snugly. Trim off the excess pastry by running a blunt knife along the rim of the tin. Prick the bottom of the pastry in several places with a fork. Spoon the cooled filling into the pastry case and level it with the back of a spoon or an offset spatula. Avoid adding a warm filling to the pastry case as the heat will melt it. If the filling is not at room temperature by the time the case is ready, chill it in the fridge until completely cool.

7. Chill the filled pastry case in the fridge for at least 30 minutes before baking it: this will prevent the sides of the tart from sagging while baking.

8. Meanwhile, place the shelf in the lowest position in the oven and preheat it to 180°C (350°F/Gas mark 4).

9. Bake for 50–55 minutes until the edges of the pastry are deep caramel in colour. Cover the top of the tart with a sheet of baking paper or foil after the first 30 minutes for a more homogeneous bake. The filling will swell and probably crack while baking, but it will settle back to its original thickness once the tart cools. Take the tart out of the oven and let it cool completely in the tin.

MAKE THE GANACHE AND ASSEMBLE

10. Place a 20–24cm (8–9½in) cake board (or a flat plate of equivalent size) over the filling and turn it upside down. Carefully lift the tin, replace it with the serving plate and turn the tart the right way up again. Remove the cake board.

11. Make the ganache: if you are using a chocolate bar, chop it into very small pieces using a sharp knife. Avoid leaving larger pieces as they will be more difficult to melt. Place the chocolate chips or chopped chocolate in a medium bowl, large enough to also accommodate the cream. In a small saucepan, bring the cream to a light simmer. When it starts simmering, remove from the heat and add the butter, stirring to melt it. Pour the hot cream over the chocolate and cover it with a plate. Let it sit for 3 minutes, then give it a good stir with a silicone spatula to combine until all the chocolate is melted. Set aside to cool. When stirring the ganache, use a folding movement rather than beating the mixture. This will avoid incorporating air bubbles which might end up spoiling the surface of the tart. When the ganache is warm to the touch and runny, pour it over the tart and level it with an offset spatula. Set aside to cool completely.

12. Meanwhile, wash and pat dry the fruit. Leave the smaller berries whole, cut the strawberries and the grapes in half lengthways, peel and slice the kiwis. Arrange the fruit around the tart as a crown and serve at room temperature. Store in the fridge for up to 2–3 days.

ALSO TRY…

To add a little bite to the filling, add 40g (⅓ cup) diced candied citrus peel and for extra crunchiness, sprinkle the semolina and ricotta layer with 30g (scant ¼ cup) chopped roasted hazelnuts before pouring over the ganache.

Torta Mimì
Mimi Cake

— gluten-free

SERVES UP TO 8

For the dacquoise
100g (3½oz) egg white (about 3 medium
eggs), at room temperature
pinch of salt
250g (1¾ cups) icing (confectioners') sugar
150g (1½ cups) ground almonds

For the buttercream
70g (2½oz) egg yolk (4–5 medium egg yolks)
50g (generous 3 tbsp) water
110g (scant ⅔ cup) caster (superfine) sugar
1 tsp vanilla bean paste
210g (scant 1 cup) unsalted butter, at room
temperature
3 tbsp Marsala wine

For the assembly
50g (⅓ cup) chopped roasted hazelnuts
unsweetened cocoa powder, for dusting

Strictly speaking, *Torta Mimì* is not an Italian
classic, and in that sense, it is the only
exception in this book. It is, however, one of
our family classics: my dad created it one day,
after realising that we had no flour in the house.
He could not possibly forego dessert after a
Sunday lunch, so he came up with this layered
cake, made of discs of almond dacquoise filled
with Marsala buttercream and hazelnuts. The
result is a phenomenally indulgent cake, very
rich and sweet, with the perfect balance of
creamy, crispy and silky textures. We loved it
so much that we named it after him: Mimì is how
everybody refers to my dad in the local dialect.

The buttercream uses pasteurised egg yolk,
so you will need a thermometer to measure the
temperature of the syrup before trickling it into
the eggs. Unfortunately, I have yet to find a reliable
method to do this without a thermometer...

This cake can be served immediately, or
made in advance, although the humidity will
soften the dacquoise over time. It is best served
at room temperature and not stored in the
fridge, where the dacquoise becomes soggy and
the silkiness of the cream might get spoiled.

MAKE THE DACQUOISE

1. Line 2 baking sheets with baking paper, then
   draw 3 discs of 18cm (7in) diameter on them
   using a plate or a cake board as a template;
   you should be able to fit 2 discs on one sheet
   and the third on the second. Set aside. Set
   2 shelves close to the middle of the oven and
   preheat it to 140°C fan (325°F/Gas mark 3).
2. Make a meringue by beating the egg whites
   and salt in the bowl of a stand mixer fitted
   with the whisk attachment on medium speed.
   When the mixture is foamy, increase the speed
   and add the sugar in 3 batches; the mixture
   will thicken after each addition. The meringue
   is ready when glossy, the peaks on the whisk
   are stiff and do not fold over, and when you
   can no longer feel the grittiness of the sugar
   when rubbing it between your fingertips (it will
   take 10–12 minutes). Fold the ground almonds
   into the meringue in 3 stages with a silicone
   spatula, then transfer it into a piping bag with
   a 10mm (½in) plain nozzle.
3. Secure the baking paper on the baking sheets
   with a smear of dacquoise, then, following

the circles on the paper, pipe 3 discs of dacquoise. Start from the outside and pipe a spiral towards the centre of each disc. Pipe small dacquoise kisses with the leftovers. Bake both sheets together for 8 minutes, then swap top and bottom and bake for a further 8 minutes. Switch off the oven, wedge a small ball of foil in the door to keep it ajar and leave the dacquoise to dry in the oven until completely cooled.

MAKE THE BUTTERCREAM

4. Meanwhile, make the buttercream: place the egg yolk in the same mixer bowl used for the meringue (no need to wash it). Place the water and sugar (in this order) in a small saucepan and bring to a simmer over a medium heat. When the syrup starts simmering, reduce the heat. Do not disturb the syrup while simmering. Monitor the temperature of the sugar syrup and when this reaches 115°C (239°F), start the mixer with the whisk attachment and beat the egg yolk at full speed. Keep simmering the syrup until it reaches 121°C (250°F); meanwhile, the egg yolk will have almost tripled in volume. Once the syrup reaches 121°C (250°F), remove it from the heat and wait until it stops bubbling. Slowly dribble it into the yolks, while the mixer is whisking. Avoid pouring the hot syrup over the spinning whisk: let it flow steadily along the inside of the bowl instead. Keep whisking the egg yolks at full speed for about 7–8 minutes until the mixture cools to room temperature. The egg yolks are ready when the mixture looks very pale, fluffy and stiff.

5. Once the mixture has cooled, add the vanilla. Dice the butter into at least 6 cubes and add

them to the bowl one by one, still whisking. Wait for each cube of butter to be fully incorporated before adding the next and scrape the sides of the bowl with a silicone spatula as necessary. The mixture will initially deflate, then it will look almost liquid. Fear not, this is normal; keep whisking and adding the butter. Once all the butter has been incorporated, let the mixer whisk the cream for a further 10 minutes until it looks very pale, stiff and creamy.

6. Finally, add the Marsala wine and whisk it for a few seconds just to incorporate it. Transfer the buttercream to a piping bag fitted with a 6mm (¼in) plain nozzle. Piping the buttercream gives the neatest result, but you can also spoon it on to the dacquoise. Avoid storing the buttercream in the fridge as it will become stiff and difficult to pipe. If you have to store it in the fridge, take it out at least 1 hour before you need it to give it time to soften.

ASSEMBLE

7. Secure one disc of dacquoise on a serving plate with a dollop of buttercream. Pipe or spoon a layer of buttercream on to the dacquoise. Scatter over half the chopped hazelnuts. Add another disc of dacquoise, a second layer of buttercream and the remaining hazelnuts. Top the stack with the last disc of dacquoise. Decorate the top of the cake with the dacquoise kisses, securing them with a smear of buttercream. Finish with a light dusting of cocoa powder. Store under a cake dome for up to 2–3 days.

Torta Caprese
Caprese Cake

— gluten-free

SERVES UP TO 14
FOR A 27CM (10¾IN), 5CM (2IN) DEEP CAKE TIN

cornflour (cornstarch), for dusting
200g (1½ cups) whole unblanched almonds
150g (5½oz) dark chocolate chips (50–55%
    cocoa solids)
40g (scant ½ cup) unsweetened
    cocoa powder
1 tsp baking powder
180g (¾ cup) unsalted butter, plus extra
    for greasing
180g (1 cup) caster (superfine) sugar
1 tsp vanilla bean paste
½ tsp natural almond extract
2 tbsp dark rum
250g (9oz) egg (about 5 medium eggs) at room
    temperature, separated
pinch of salt
icing (confectioners') sugar, for dusting

Torta Caprese owes its name to the beautiful
and romantic island of Capri, just off the coast
of Naples, from which it originates. The recipe
is naturally gluten-free: in fact, the story goes
that this cake is the result of a mistake made
at the beginning of the 20th century by a local
chef who, in a hurry, forgot to add flour to his
batter. The result is a light and flavoursome cake
with a crispy, delicate skin and a moist centre.

Some modern variations use ready-
made ground almonds, but I find that blitzing
whole unblanched almonds together with the
chocolate chips delivers a better, more rustic,
texture while preserving the freshness and
flavour of the nuts. For a deeper flavour, you
can also roast the almonds in the oven for
6–8 minutes at 180°C fan (400°F/Gas mark 6).
In this case, allow them to cool completely
before blitzing them.

Torta Caprese is traditionally baked in
a deep tart tin with smooth, flaring sides, but
it may be baked equally well in a standard
springform tin. It is served upside down, coated
in a thick layer of icing sugar, often decorated
with a stencil. This cake is delicious on its own,
but it goes particularly well with a drizzle of
pouring cream or smothered with a generous
dollop of orange marmalade or raspberry jam.

1. Set the shelf in the middle of the oven and
    preheat it to 170°C (340°F/Gas mark 3).
    Grease the bottom and sides of the tin with
    butter and dust with cornflour. I recommend
    also lining the bottom of the tin with a disc
    of baking paper as this will ensure a smoother
    cake top.
2. Grind the almonds and chocolate chips in
    a food processor at high speed for about
    1 minute until the mixture looks gritty. It is fine
    to leave some coarser bits of almond in the
    mix: these will give the cake a pleasant bite.
3. Sift the cocoa powder and the baking powder
    into the almond and chocolate mixture and
    combine well with a spoon. Set aside for later.
    On a warm day, the dry mixture might clump
    up, so make sure that all clumps are broken
    up before moving on to the next step.
4. Soften the butter in the microwave until
    creamy but not liquid; 10–20 seconds should
    be enough (see page 9). Add the softened
    butter to the bowl of a stand mixer fitted with
    the whisk attachment. Add half of the sugar,
    the vanilla, almond extract and rum, and whisk

the mixture until soft and creamy. Start at very low speed and gradually increase to full speed as the butter softens. Incorporate the egg yolks one at a time and keep beating at high speed until pale and fluffy. Set aside.

5. In a separate bowl, beat the egg whites with the salt using a handheld electric whisk until foamy. Gradually add the remaining sugar to the egg whites and keep beating to make a stiff meringue. Do not over-beat the whites or it will be more difficult to incorporate them into the batter: the meringue should form stiff, shiny peaks but not look dry and clumpy.

6. Add one third of the dry mixture and one large spoonful of meringue to the yolk and butter cream and keep folding until well combined. Repeat twice more until all the dry mixture has been added. Incorporate the remaining meringue, gently folding it into the batter.

7. Pour the batter into the prepared tin, gently flatten the top and immediately bake for 55 minutes–1 hour or until a skewer inserted into the centre of the cake comes out clean. Don't be tempted to over-bake this cake: the skin should be crispy, but the core should remain moist. Leave the cake to cool in the tin on a wire rack for about 1 hour.

8. Pass a blunt knife around the sides of the tin and turn the cake upside down over a cooling rack to cool completely. Transfer to a serving plate and dust with a generous amount of icing sugar. You can add a simple but effective finish by placing a few fabric ribbons over the cake and using them as stencils before dusting it with icing sugar. Store under a cake dome for up to 3–4 days or freeze for up to a month.

ALSO TRY…

The best bakeries in Naples serve *Torta Caprese* as individual servings baked in hemispherical moulds, so why not give it a try?

Tiramisù

— nut-free

SERVES UP TO 20
FOR A 30CM (12IN) SERVING BOWL

For the savoiardi
Prepare one batch of *savoiardi* using the
quantities and methods on pages 85–6.
Savoiardi can be prepared up to a week in
advance and stored in an airtight container
until needed. Alternatively, you will need
a 200g (7oz) pack of store-bought *savoiardi*.

For the coffee syrup
250g (generous 1 cup) strong espresso
    coffee (decaf works equally well)
40g (¼ cup) caster (superfine) sugar

For the cream filling
120g (4¼oz) egg yolk (about 7–8 medium egg
    yolks), at room temperature
50g (3½ tbsp) water
200g (generous 1 cup) caster (superfine) sugar
500g (2¼ cups) mascarpone, cold
300g (1⅓ cups) whipping (heavy) cream
    (35–40% fat), cold

To decorate
50g (½ cup) unsweetened cocoa powder

Nothing says Italian dessert more than tiramisù.
In its original form, it is incredibly easy to
make and so decadently sweet that it is almost
impossible not to love. It is also the very first
'cake' that most children learn how to make as,
with a pack of shop-bought *savoiardi*, there is
nothing to bake, shape or decorate...

The original recipe uses unpasteurised
eggs, often with the yolks and whites whipped
separately, then mixed with mascarpone. I have
never felt comfortable feeding raw eggs to my
kids though, so I have been using a version of
this dessert that pasteurises the yolks with a hot
sugary syrup, making it safer for most.

The ingredients list includes a batch
of *savoiardi* biscuits, which you can either
buy pre-made or make with my recipe. I
particularly like the contrast between the sweet
mascarpone cream and the bitter coffee, so
I keep my syrup relatively low in sugar. However,
if you would rather go for a sweeter overall
effect, you can dissolve up to 100g (generous
½ cup) sugar in the hot coffee.

I recommend only dusting the top of
tiramisù with unsweetened cocoa powder just
before serving it. If you do it any earlier, the
cocoa will absorb moisture from the cream and
look wet and splotchy. Tiramisù must rest in the
fridge overnight for the cream to stiffen up and
acquire the right consistency, and to give time
for the coffee syrup to soak the *savoiardi* layers.
Even after resting, tiramisù is very much a trifle-
like dessert, so serve it spooned into bowls: this
is not the right stuff for neatly cut slices!

MAKE THE COFFEE SYRUP

1. Pour the coffee into a shallow, flat-bottomed
   bowl, slightly larger than the largest *savoiardi*.
   A cereal bowl works perfectly. Dissolve the
   sugar in the hot coffee and leave to cool.

MAKE THE CREAM FILLING

2. Place the egg yolk in the bowl of a stand mixer
   fitted with the whisk attachment.

CAKES & TARTS

3. Place the water and sugar (in this order) in a small saucepan and bring to a simmer over a medium heat. When the syrup starts simmering, reduce the heat. Do not disturb the syrup while simmering: this will minimise the possibility of the sugar crystallising. Monitor the temperature of the sugar syrup and when this reaches 115°C (239°F), start the mixer to beat the egg yolk at full speed.

4. Keep simmering the syrup until it reaches 121°C (250°F); meanwhile, the egg yolk will have almost tripled in volume. Once the syrup reaches 121°C (250°F), remove it from the heat and wait until it stops bubbling. Slowly dribble it into the yolk, while the mixer is whisking. Avoid pouring the hot syrup over the spinning whisk: let it flow steadily along the inside of the bowl instead. Keep whisking the egg yolk at full speed for about 12 minutes until the mixture cools to room temperature.

5. Meanwhile, place the mascarpone and cream in a medium bowl and whip the mixture with a handheld electric whisk. Start slowly to roughly combine the cheese and cream, then increase the speed to maximum. Whip the mixture to stiff peaks for 2 minutes until it looks completely dull.

6. Remove the bowl from the stand mixer and whisk one third of the yolk mixture into the whipped mascarpone and cream to loosen it. Add the remaining yolk mixture and gently fold it in.

ASSEMBLE

7. Arrange the *savoiardi*, the bowl with coffee syrup and the mascarpone cream near the serving bowl. Dip the *savoiardi*, one at a time, into the coffee syrup, then place them in the serving bowl, arranging them so that they form a regular, continuous layer of sponge at the bottom of the bowl. They must not be kept in the coffee for any longer than a few seconds or they will disintegrate. Even though they will look dry at first, enough moisture will soften them while the dessert is resting.

8. Pour or spoon half of the mascarpone cream over the *savoiardi* layer and level it out with the back of a spoon. Arrange a second layer of coffee-soaked *savoiardi* over the mascarpone cream. Pour or spoon the remaining mascarpone cream over the second layer of *savoiardi*, levelling it out with the back of a spoon. For a fancier finish, pipe over dollops of cream with an 8mm (⅜in) nozzle. Cover the bowl with clingfilm and leave in the fridge to rest overnight.

DECORATE

9. Generously dust the top of the mascarpone cream with cocoa powder just before serving. Store in the fridge for up to 2 days.

ALSO TRY...

For an alcoholic version, add 40g (scant 3 tbsp) white rum or coffee liqueur to the coffee syrup, once this has cooled to room temperature, and add 2 tablespoons of dry Marsala wine to the mascarpone cream.

Mimosa ai Lamponi
Raspberry Mimosa

— nut-free

SERVES UP TO 20
FOR A 25CM (10IN) SPRINGFORM CAKE TIN

For the pan di Spagna

320g (11¼oz) egg (about 6 medium eggs)
200g (generous 1 cup) caster (superfine) sugar
2 tsp vanilla bean paste
zest of 1 organic lemon
2 tsp red or ruby colouring gel
100g (1 cup) soft wheat 00 flour
100g (1 cup) cornflour (cornstarch)

For the raspberry diplomat cream

500g (2 cups) whole milk
1 tsp vanilla bean paste
zest of 1 organic lemon
75g (2½oz) egg yolk (about 5 medium egg yolks)
110g (scant ⅔ cup) caster (superfine) sugar
50g (½ cup) cornflour (cornstarch)
small pinch of salt
300g (10½oz) fresh raspberries
300g (1⅓ cups) whipping (heavy) cream
    (35−40% fat), cold
80g (generous ½ cup) icing
    (confectioners') sugar

For the fragolino syrup

170g (scant ¾ cup) water
60g (⅓ cup) caster (superfine) sugar
60g (¼ cup) fragolino or wild strawberry liqueur

For the assembly

a few mint leaves and shoots (optional)

Mimosa cake is a nationwide tradition, typically gifted to women on 8 March to celebrate International Women's Day. In its simplest form, it is made with a *pan di Spagna* sponge (pages 72−8), doused with a sweet syrup and filled with diplomat cream. Despite the sophisticated name, diplomat cream is simply a mix of pastry cream and sweet whipped cream: the result is a super soft and extremely delicate filling, perfect on its own, but outrageously good when mixed with fresh fruit.

Our family's favourite combination includes fresh raspberries and a syrup flavoured with fragolino liqueur, a sweet spirit infused with wild strawberries. Although deceptively simple to make, this impressive cake is not only irresistible, but also extremely elegant.

MAKE THE PAN DI SPAGNA

1. Prepare and bake the *pan di Spagna* following the method on pages 74−5. Before adding both flours to the *pan di Spagna* batter, whisk the food colouring gel into the whipped egg mixture until fully incorporated. To achieve a deep and striking colour, use a good-quality gel. Avoid liquid food colouring as this alters the texture of the batter and is usually less effective than gel.

MAKE THE RASPBERRY DIPLOMAT CREAM

2. Make the pastry cream following the method on pages 204−6.
3. While the pastry cream cools, wash, drain and pat the raspberries dry with kitchen paper. Roughly chop them into large pieces, so that

each berry is sliced into no more than 2–3 pieces. Place in a medium bowl and set aside.

4. Pour the cold whipping cream into the bowl of a stand mixer fitted with the whisk attachment. Add the icing sugar and start whisking on low speed to combine. Increase the speed to high and keep whisking until the cream starts to thicken and the whisk leaves visible marks in the cream. Reduce the mixer speed to medium and keep a close eye on the cream surface. As soon as the cream goes from shiny to completely dull, stop the mixer. This should take 2–3 minutes.

5. Once the pastry cream is at room temperature, make the diplomat cream by incorporating the whipped cream into it gently, folding in one large spoonful at a time. The pastry cream will have probably become rather stiff upon cooling, especially if stored in the fridge. Beat it energetically with a spoon or a handheld electric whisk until soft, lump-free and creamy before incorporating the whipped cream.

6. Spoon one third of the diplomat cream into the bowl with the chopped raspberries and gently fold in the fruit: this will be used for filling the cake. Set aside the remaining two thirds of diplomat cream, which will be used to coat the cake.

MAKE THE FRAGOLINO SYRUP

7. Place the water and sugar (in this order) into a small saucepan and warm it gently, just enough to dissolve the sugar. When the sugar is fully dissolved, remove from the heat and set aside to cool. When the syrup is at room temperature, add the fragolino liqueur and stir.

ASSEMBLE

8. Slice the *pan di Spagna* sponge into 3 equal discs. People with good dexterity can cut 3 perfect discs with a bread knife, but I am not one of those and I cannot recommend a cake slicer enough. Trim the darker skin off the middle disc and discard it so that you are left with a disc of bright red sponge. Dice this sponge into 8–10mm (3/8–1/2in) cubes and set aside to decorate the cake.

9. Secure one of the two remaining discs, cut side (i.e. crumb) up, on a serving plate with a small dollop of cream. Douse the bottom disc with half the syrup, using a pastry brush or a spoon. Spoon the diplomat cream with raspberries over the soaked sponge and shape it into a dome with a small spatula.

10. Trim off about 1cm (1/2in) around the circumference of the remaining sponge disc, so that it is slightly smaller than the bottom disc, and place it over the domed filling, cut side up. Soak this second disc with the remaining syrup.

11. Coat the whole cake with the diplomat cream (without raspberries) to give it a domed shape. There is no need to smooth it down perfectly as this layer will be hidden by the decoration. Carefully arrange the cubes of sponge over the cream-covered cake. Start from the top of the cake and work your way down the sides until you have covered the entire cake. The cubes will stick easily to the diplomat cream with a gentle push. Decorate the top of the cake with a couple of mint shoots and fresh leaves, if you like. Store in the fridge for up to 2–3 days.

CAKES & TARTS

GIUSEPPE'S ITALIAN BAKES

Crostata di Frutta
Fruit Tart

— nut-free

SERVES UP TO 16
FOR A 30CM (12IN) TART TIN

For the orange cream filling
400g (1¾ cups) whole milk
1 tsp vanilla bean paste
zest of 1 organic lemon
60g (2¼oz) egg yolk (about 4 medium egg yolks)
90g (½ cup) caster (superfine) sugar
40g (generous ⅓ cup) cornflour (cornstarch)
small pinch of salt
80g (⅓ cup) freshly squeezed orange juice
zest of 1 organic orange

For the *pasta frolla* pastry
300g (1⅓ cups) soft wheat 00 flour, plus extra
    for dusting
150g (⅔ cup) unsalted butter, cold, plus extra
    for greasing
100g (¾ cup) icing (confectioners') sugar
70g (2½oz) egg (about 1 medium egg and
    1 yolk), cold
zest of 1 organic lemon
1 tsp vanilla bean paste
pinch of salt
80g (2¾oz) white chocolate chips or bar

For the fruit topping
50g (1¾oz) fresh blueberries
50g (1¾oz) fresh raspberries
50g (1¾oz) fresh blackberries
150g (5½oz) fresh grapes
2 fresh kiwis
100g (3½oz) fresh strawberries
2 fresh oranges

For the glaze
3.5g platinum grade gelatine leaves (about
    2 leaves, see page 12)
60g (⅓ cup) caster (superfine) sugar
1 tbsp cornflour (cornstarch)
150g (scant ⅔ cup) water

There is something regal about a tart covered with carefully arranged, glistening, almost jewel-like pieces of fresh fruit: this colourful crown can easily take centre stage at the most sophisticated dinner party, but it is equally at home in the smallest family celebration.

The traditional *crostata di frutta* is made with simple vanilla pastry cream, however, I have added a delicate and tangy orange flavour to mine for an even lighter and fresher aftertaste. The making process might look daunting, but the big advantage of this dessert is that all individual elements can be prepared in advance, so the tart only needs assembling at the last minute.

I seal the *pasta frolla* base with a thin layer of white chocolate: not only does its sweetness complement the acidity of the fruit, but it also stops the humidity of the topping from turning the pastry soggy. Overall, this pastry will need about 600g (1lb 5oz) of fresh fruit for the decoration; pick fruits according to your and your family's tastes: berries always work very well, soft pulp fruits like mango or kiwi are ideal, but watery fruits like pears or watermelons are best avoided. Bananas are a perfect addition, as long as they are sliced and marinated in pure lemon juice to stop them from browning.

Store this tart in the fridge once decorated and serve it cold.

MAKE THE CREAM FILLING

1. Make the orange pastry cream following the method on page 206. The cream filling should be prepared at least 1–2 hours before it is needed to give it time to cool to room temperature. The pastry should never be filled with warm cream.

MAKE THE PASTRY CASING

2. Prepare the *pasta frolla* following the method on page 217. *Pasta frolla* can be prepared up to a couple of days in advance and stored wrapped in clingfilm in the fridge until needed.
3. Grease and flour the tin well, including the sides. Line the bottom of the tin with a disc of baking paper.
4. Take the pastry out of the fridge, unwrap it and roll it to a thickness of 5mm (¼in) over a well-floured worktop, shaping it into a disc. Wrap the pastry around the rolling pin and unroll it over the prepared tin. Gently press the pastry into the tin so that it fits snugly. Trim off the excess pastry by running a blunt knife along the rim of the tin. Place in the fridge to cool for 30 minutes.
5. Meanwhile, place the shelf in the middle of the oven and preheat it to 180°C (350°F/ Gas mark 4).
6. Take the rested pastry out of the fridge and pierce a few holes in the bottom of the casing with a fork. Line the bottom and sides of the pastry casing with one sheet of baking paper and hold it down with ceramic beans. Try to use a single sheet of paper to line the pastry case, as this will make it easier to remove the

hot beans during baking. Spread the ceramic beans evenly across the bottom of the casing, all the way up to the sides. Old, dry pulses, such as lentils, beans or chickpeas, or rice, can be used instead of ceramic beans but be aware that you will no longer be able to cook them once they have been baked.

7. Bake the pastry casing for 15 minutes, then lift out the beans with the baking paper, and put it back in the oven for a further 8–10 minutes. The casing is ready when the bottom starts to turn golden. Remove the pastry case from the oven and let it cool completely in the tin. Once at room temperature, take it out of the tin and move it on to a serving plate.
8. If you are using a white chocolate bar instead of chips, roughly chop it into small pieces. Place the chips or pieces of chocolate in a microwave-safe bowl and microwave it for 30 seconds first, then in subsequent 10-second bursts until the chocolate is melted. Mix the chocolate energetically between bursts to distribute the heat evenly. Brush a thin layer of white chocolate over the entire pastry base with a pastry brush. Let it set.

PREPARE THE FRUIT TOPPING

9. Wash the fruit and pat it dry with kitchen paper. Leave the smaller berries whole, cut the grapes in half lengthways, peel and slice the kiwis and slice the strawberries. Segment the orange by completely slicing off the skin (both rind and pith), then remove each segment by slicing with a sharp paring knife along the membranes that separate the segments. Remove the seeds, if needed.

CAKES & TARTS

ASSEMBLE

10. Spoon or pipe the cream filling into the pastry casing and level it with the back of a spoon or a small offset spatula. Arrange the fruit over the cream filling: start by covering the edges of the pastry casing, then move towards the centre, laying the fruit in concentric circles until the whole tart is decorated.

GLAZE

11. Soak the gelatine leaves in a bowl of cold water for 10 minutes.
12. Meanwhile, place the sugar and cornflour in a small saucepan and whisk them together until fully combined. Add the water and bring to a gentle simmer over a low heat. Simmer for 1 minute, then remove from the heat and wait for the syrup to stop boiling.
13. Lift the gelatine leaves from the water, squeeze out any excess water and drop them into the hot syrup. Whisk well to dissolve the gelatine completely. Coat the pieces of fruit, one by one, by gently brushing the warm glaze with a pastry brush. Only dab the small berries with the brush to avoid misplacing them. You only need a thin layer of glaze to coat the fruit; avoid being too generous as, once set, the glaze is slightly hazy and it might ruin the overall appearance of the tart if the coating is too thick. Store in the fridge for up to 2 days.

ALSO TRY...

This tart tastes its best when decorated with ripe fruit in season, however, canned apricots, peaches or pineapples work extremely well too, making it also suitable for a winter celebration.

Babbà al Rum
Rum Baba

— nut-free

SERVES UP TO 14
FOR A 24CM (9½IN) *BABBÀ* MOULD

For the sponge
200g (scant 1½ cups) strong bread flour
    (14–15% protein content), cold
20g (generous 1 tbsp) caster (superfine) sugar
1 tsp dry yeast
200g (7oz) egg (about 4 medium eggs), cold
½ tsp salt
1 tsp vanilla bean paste
60g (¼ cup) unsalted butter, plus extra for
    greasing, at room temperature

For the syrup
peel of 2 organic lemons
peel of 2 organic oranges
1.5kg (6½ cups) water
700g (scant 4 cups) caster (superfine) sugar
1 cinnamon stick
2 star anise
250g (generous 1 cup) dark rum

For the decoration
100g (3½oz) apricot jam
200g (scant 1 cup) whipping (heavy) cream
    (35–40% fat), cold
40g (¼ cup) icing (confectioners') sugar
½ tsp vanilla bean paste
150g (5½oz) mixed fresh fruit, such as 1 fig,
    2 strawberries, 1 kiwi and 4 blackberries

The best compliment anybody can give you in Naples is '*sì nù babbà*', literally: 'you are a *babbà*'. That is how much this cake is engrained in local culture. The origins date back to 18th-century Poland, but this dessert was perfected in France before becoming almost the symbol of Naples, where today it is so ubiquitous to be considered practically a street food, when baked in its characteristic small, mushroom-shaped, single-serving format.

However, nothing screams 'centrepiece' more than a majestic *babbà* cake, baked in the typical flared tin with scalloped sides, coated in shimmering apricot glaze and decorated with swirls of luscious Chantilly cream and fresh fruit: this truly is the royalty of Italian baking. I find it absolutely staggering that something so theatrical and imposing can be made with a very short list of everyday ingredients: as is often the case, it's all in the method! No fancy equipment is needed either, other than a good stand mixer and perhaps a curved plastic scraper to help with handling the sticky dough.

Babbà has the undeserved reputation of being difficult to tackle; probably because of the manual method used in the olden days, which made its preparation a gargantuan task. Today, the mixer does all the work, and the process is much simpler and more controllable. It is, however, still a long procedure: the main unlisted ingredient of *babbà* remains time, albeit, I would argue, it is time well spent.

I bake my *babbà* cakes in the traditional mould; however, any gugelhupf or bundt tin would work as well, as long as they have a conic hole in the middle to guarantee a good heat distribution; I would stay clear of moulds with very intricate shapes or deeply embossed as the sponge is more likely to get stuck. The sponge can be made and soaked on the same day, although it is best to bake it the day before and let it dry overnight. The baked sponge can be stored unwrapped at room temperature for up to 3 days before being soaked, and it can also be frozen, wrapped in clingfilm, and thawed at room temperature for 24 hours before soaking it in syrup.

If handling a large *babbà* cake sounds daunting, start with a set of small ones: soaking those in syrup is easier than soaking a large cake. The quantities below will make eight 60g (2¼oz) single-serving *babbà*: check the 'Also try...' section for full details.

MAKE THE SPONGE

1. At least 30 minutes before starting the dough, place the eggs in fridge, the flour in the freezer and keep the butter at room temperature. This is an unmissable step as cold ingredients will counterbalance the inevitable warming of the dough due to the vigorous beating in the mixer. A warm dough would melt the butter, when it is added, and make its incorporation more difficult. The butter, on the other hand, should be at room temperature as this gives it the perfect texture to be effectively and gradually incorporated into the dough.

2. Place the flour in the bowl of a stand mixer fitted with the paddle attachment. Add the sugar and yeast and mix with a spoon until fully combined. Weigh the eggs in a spouted jug. Start the mixer on medium speed and add the eggs gradually, roughly one at a time. Wait for each egg to be fully incorporated before adding more. Take your time to do this: adding the eggs should take about 2 minutes. Then add the salt and vanilla, increase the speed to high and work the dough for 8–10 minutes or until it wraps around the paddle and comes

cleanly off the sides of the bowl. This stage is critical as it will develop the strong network of gluten which is what keeps the structure of the *babbà* together even once fully soaked.

3. Meanwhile, prepare the butter by dicing it into 6 cubes. Grease a large bowl with a light coating of butter. This bowl will be used for proving the dough so it needs to be large enough to accommodate at least twice the volume of the dough.

4. Once the dough is ready, stop the mixer, scrape the sides of the bowl with a curved plastic scraper and swap the paddle attachment for the hook. Start the mixer again on a high speed and add the butter, one cube at a time. Wait for each cube of butter to be almost fully incorporated before adding the next. This will take a further 6–8 minutes.

5. Butter your hands and the scraper, scoop the dough out of the mixer bowl, scraping the sides, and transfer it to the proving bowl. The dough will look silky and shiny, and it will feel soft, elastic and surprisingly stringy. When you stretch a bit of dough between your fingers, it should form a very thin, almost veil-like membrane without tearing. Professionals perform this 'windowpane test' to check the status of the dough: if successful, it is a sign that the process has worked, and you are on your way to a perfect *babbà*. A bit of a warning: do not even attempt handling this dough with dry hands as it is one of the stickiest substances known to humankind!

6. Cover the proving bowl with clingfilm and transfer it to the oven, with the shelf set in the middle. Place a small tray on the bottom of the oven and fill it with boiling water. Avoid placing the tray with boiling water right beneath the

dough, but place the two in opposite corners of the oven. Close the oven and leave the dough to prove until doubled in volume: it should take about 1 hour. The boiling water creates a warm and humid environment in your oven maintaining the temperature between 30°C (86°F) and 40°C (104°F), which speeds up the proving stage significantly. If you decide not to use the hot water trick, this first proving will take about 2 hours.

7. While the dough is proving, thoroughly coat the mould with a thin layer of butter. It is best not to flour it as this would spoil the appearance of the sponge, once baked.

8. Butter your hands, the worktop and the scraper. Drop the proved dough on to the buttered worktop, stretch it and fold it in half a few times to deflate it. The dough will be very wet and sticky, so a scraper is almost essential. Give the dough a roughly round shape and push a finger in the middle to make a hole, then gently place it in the buttered mould, sliding the central cone of the mould into the hole. The dough should take up no more than one third of the mould volume as it will swell significantly while proving and baking.

9. Cover the mould with clingfilm, place it back in the oven, and wait until the dough is 2cm (¾in) or less from the top of the mould; this should take about 1 hour 20 minutes–1½ hours. You can leave the tray with warm water in the oven at this stage as it will speed up the proving.

10. Take the mould and the tray with water out of the oven, but keep the dough covered. Set the shelf in the lowest position in the oven and preheat it to 180°C (350°F/Gas mark 4).

11. When the oven reaches the set temperature, remove the clingfilm and bake the *babbà* for

28–30 minutes, or until the top surface is a deep caramel colour and a skewer inserted into the deepest part of the mould comes out clean. Take the *babbà* out of the oven and turn it on to a cooling rack immediately. Leave it to cool completely, upside down and uncovered, for a few hours but preferably overnight. You can leave the *babbà* to rest uncovered for up to 2 days before soaking it: the sponge will dry out fully, ready to absorb the syrup.

MAKE THE SYRUP, THE APRICOT GLAZE AND THE CHANTILLY CREAM

12. Peel the lemons and oranges, making sure to shave only the waxy skin, leaving the white pith on the fruits. Place the water, sugar, citrus peel, cinnamon and star anise in a large pan, cover it and bring to the boil over a medium-high heat. Once boiling, reduce the heat and let it simmer for 10–15 minutes. Take off the heat and let the syrup cool in the lidded pan to about 60°C (140°F).

13. While the syrup cools, prepare the apricot glaze: place the apricot jam in a small heatproof bowl, add 2 tablespoons of the syrup, stir to combine and set aside.

14. Prepare the Chantilly cream following the method on page 75, place it in a piping bag with a 12mm (½in) star nozzle, seal the tip and the back with plastic clips and store in the fridge until needed.

15. When the syrup is at around 60°C (140°F), discard the cinnamon stick and star anise. Remove the peel and set it aside. Add the rum: the syrup is now ready to soak the sponge.

SOAK THE BABBÀ

16. Place the dry *babbà* back in its mould and pierce several holes across the surface by pushing a long skewer all the way to the bottom. You will notice that the *babbà* has shrunk and is now smaller than the mould: this is normal as the sponge has dried out and it will swell again upon soaking. Using a ladle, slowly pour the warm syrup over the *babbà* until the mould is almost full. Leave the *babbà* to soak in the mould for 5–10 minutes. Occasionally push the sponge down very gently so the bottom of the *babbà* gets fully soaked. Place a tray with tall sides over the *babbà* and use it to hold the sponge in place while you tilt the mould to pour the excess syrup back into the pan. Turn the mould over completely, so you now have the *babbà* on the tray. Pour the syrup back over the babbà with the ladle and leave it to soak in the tray for a further 5-10 minutes.

17. Place a cooling rack over a roasting tray, then carefully lift the soaked sponge out of the pan and place it over the cooling rack to drain. Gently but firmly, squeeze out the excess syrup by pressing the sponge between your hands, moving them progressively around the crown of the *babbà*. Lift the *babbà* with a couple of long spatulas or with a cake lifter and place it on a serving plate. At this stage, the *babbà* is at its weakest, so handle it carefully to avoid breaking.

DECORATE

18. Warm the glaze in a microwave until it is runny enough to be brushed. It should take about 30 seconds in a 800W microwave. The glaze should be smooth and free of fruit chunks. If your jam contains fruit pieces, push it through a sieve with the back of a spoon while warm.

19. Using a pastry brush, coat the entire surface of the *babbà* with the apricot glaze. If necessary, warm it up for a few seconds in a microwave to loosen it. Pipe the Chantilly cream around the base and over the top of the crown.

20. Arrange the fresh fruit over the top to decorate. Slice the citrus peel used for the syrup into thin strips and add them too. Store in the fridge for up to 2 days. The baked sponge (unsoaked) can be frozen for up to a month.

ALSO TRY…

To make small, single-serving *babbà*, follow the same method as for the cake but divide the dough into eight 60g (2¼oz) pieces, then drop them into well-buttered 125ml (4fl oz) pots for the second proving. Bake them on the middle shelf of the oven for 10 minutes at 200°C (400°F/Gas mark 6), then 10 minutes at 180°C (350°F/Gas mark 4).

The syrup in this recipe is seriously boozy and for adults only; however, the rum can be completely omitted from the syrup for a non-alcoholic version and drizzled neat only over the individual slices of those who want it.

Torta di Pan di Spagna
Celebration Cake

SERVES UP TO 20
FOR A 25CM (10IN) SPRINGFORM CAKE TIN

For the pan di Spagna
butter, for greasing
320g (11¼oz) egg (about 6 medium eggs),
 at room temperature
200g (generous 1 cup) caster (superfine) sugar
2 tsp vanilla bean paste
zest of 1 organic lemon
100g (1 cup) soft wheat 00 flour
100g (1 cup) cornflour (cornstarch)

For the orange cream filling
1 organic lemon
700g (2¾ cups) whole milk
2 tsp vanilla bean paste
100g (3½oz) egg yolk (about 6–7 medium
 egg yolks)
150g (generous ¾ cup) caster (superfine) sugar
70g (¾ cup) cornflour (cornstarch)
small pinch of salt
100g (scant ½ cup) freshly squeezed
 orange juice
zest of 1 organic orange
½ tsp natural orange extract
2 tbsp triple sec liqueur (optional)

For the amaretto syrup
300g (1¼ cups + 1 tbsp) water
100g (generous ½ cup) caster (superfine) sugar
40g (3 tbsp) amaretto liqueur

For the Chantilly cream
800g (3¾ cups) whipping (heavy) cream
 (35–40% fat), cold
130g (scant 1 cup) icing (confectioners')
 sugar
2 tsp vanilla bean paste

For the decoration (optional)
20 whole almonds
4 dried orange slices, halved

The queen of all Italian cakes and unsurprisingly what most Italians think of as the quintessential birthday cake is based on a traditional Italian sponge... named after Spain! *Pan di Spagna* (literally: 'bread of Spain') is a sponge based only on eggs, sugar and flour: it does not include any fat or raising agent, and its loftiness is entirely dependent on the small air bubbles in the mix, which are expanded and set by the heat in the oven while baking.

It seems that the name is due to the links that the baker who invented this sponge in the early 18th century had in Spain through his master, a Genoese aristocrat who spent a few years in Madrid. The recipe is similar to génoise sponge and there are infinite theories as to which came first, and which features characterise each recipe. I will stay out of the debate and present you the version that my dad and my extended family have always used.

My *pan di Spagna* is based on three layers of sponge, soaked in a sweet syrup, alternated with layers of pastry cream and elegantly smothered in Chantilly cream. This used to be the typical format for a traditional birthday cake before sugar paste decorations took over; however, the all-white look and the very delicate texture make it an ideal wedding cake too.

The following recipe will make a *pan di Spagna* cake filled with orange cream and soaked in amaretto syrup, however the method is structured so you can pick and choose alternative flavour combinations for the sponge

and the filling to customise your own cake. Recommended matches are listed and detailed in the 'Also try...' section (page 78), but the assembly is the same whichever flavours you choose. Each individual element of this cake (sponge, cream filling, syrup) can be prepared in advance and stored in the fridge until assembly, but the Chantilly cream is best prepared just before decorating the cake. Being made with fresh dairy, this cake should be stored in the fridge and only removed just before serving.

The top of this cake traditionally includes greetings or dedications written by piping coloured gels or chocolate over the white background of the Chantilly cream. It can also be decorated with custom prints on edible paper or tempered chocolate mouldings. Shop-bought wafer or rice paper decorations are usually suitable too; however, Chantilly is not ideal for fresh fondant decorations as the humidity of the whipped cream may melt the sugar or leach some of the colour out.

MAKE THE PAN DI SPAGNA

1. Set the shelf in the bottom half of the oven so that the top of the tin sits just below the middle of the oven. Preheat it to 180°C (350°F/Gas mark 4). Grease the bottom and sides of the tin and line it with baking paper. If the tin sides are shorter than 8cm (3¼in), use a strip of paper at least 8cm (3¼in) wide to line the sides. This will ensure that no batter will spill out while baking.

2. Prepare the *pan di Spagna* batter: out of the many techniques, the most practical is the 'cold' method, where the eggs are whipped with the sugar at room temperature in a stand mixer fitted with the whisk attachment. If you have access to a good-quality and powerful stand mixer, I recommend this method: the mixer does all the work for you and you will only have one bowl to wash at the end. You must use eggs at room temperature: add them to the bowl of the stand mixer with the sugar, vanilla and lemon zest, then mix at high speed for at least 14-16 minutes until the mixture has tripled in volume and looks pale, stiff and fluffy. The mixture is ready when a blob or a ribbon dropped from the spatula back into the bowl leaves a trail that does not disappear. You can then jump directly to step 6 in the method.

3. If you don't have a stand mixer, you can use a handheld electric whisk to make *pan di Spagna* too. Prepare a bain-marie by bringing 5cm (2in) of water to a simmer in a large pan and selecting a metal bowl to fit on top of the pan without touching the water.

4. While the water heats up, add the eggs, sugar, vanilla and lemon zest to the metal bowl. When the water is ready, reduce the heat to the lowest possible setting, place the metal bowl over the gently simmering water and, using a handheld electric whisk, whisk the mixture at full speed until it reaches 50°C (122°F).

5. Once the temperature reaches 50°C (122°F), remove the bowl from the pan and keep whisking until the mixture is below 30°C (86°F); by this time the mixture will have tripled in volume and will leave a trail that does not disappear when dropped from the spatula back into the bowl. The whisking process should take no less than 15–20 minutes: do not be tempted to stop until the mixture looks very fluffy and full of air. Bear in mind that there are no chemicals in this sponge to inflate

it: the longer you whisk it for, the fluffier the final result will be.

6. Sift both flours into the egg mixture in 3 stages and fold in each addition very gently, using a silicone spatula, until just incorporated. Do not over-mix to avoid deflating the batter. Do not skip the sifting if you want to avoid clumps of flour in the sponge. I find that a handheld flour sifter is an ideal tool for this job. When folding the batter, make sure to scrape the bottom of the bowl, which is where the flour will very often clump.

7. Immediately pour the batter into the prepared tin and level the surface with a spoon or spatula. Do not shake or tap the tin to avoid knocking the air out. Bake for 35–40 minutes, or until a skewer inserted into the centre of the cake comes out clean. The sponge should be springy, and the edges should be slightly detached from the sides of the tin. If you wish to check the status of the bake midway, make sure that you do not open the oven during the first 30 minutes, or the sponge might collapse.

8. Remove from the oven and let the cake cool for 5 minutes, then remove the ring from the springform tin and let it cool for a further 5 minutes. The sponge will slightly deflate and lose any dome it might have formed in the oven: this is to be expected and it will not compromise the structure of the sponge. Turn the sponge upside down on to a cooling rack, remove the base of the tin, peel off the baking paper and let it cool completely.

9. If you are not using the sponge straight away, once at room temperature, wrap it in clingfilm and store it in the fridge until needed. The sponge can also be frozen and thawed in the fridge for 24 hours before assembling.

MAKE THE ORANGE CREAM FILLING

10. Prepare one batch of orange cream following the method on page 206. The cream filling should be prepared at least 1–2 hours before it is needed to give it time to cool to room temperature.

MAKE THE SYRUP

11. Place the water and sugar in a small pan and heat gently, stirring until the sugar is dissolved; the mixture does not need to boil. Remove from the heat and let it cool for a couple of minutes. Finally, add the amaretto and set aside to cool completely.

MAKE THE CHANTILLY CREAM

12. Pour the cold cream into the bowl of a stand mixer fitted with the whisk attachment. Add the icing sugar and vanilla and start whisking on low speed to combine. Increase the speed to high and keep whisking until the cream starts to thicken and the whisk leaves visible marks in the cream. Reduce the speed to medium and mix until the surface of the cream goes from shiny to completely dull. It will take about 2–3 minutes.

13. Spoon the cream into a piping bag with a 10mm (½in) stainless-steel star nozzle, seal the back and the tip of the piping bag with plastic clips and store in the fridge until ready to use.

ASSEMBLE

14. Slice the sponge into 3 discs of equal thickness. People with good dexterity can cut 3 perfect discs with a bread knife, but I am not one

of those and so I recommend a cake slicer. Smudge some cream filling on the serving plate to secure the sponge and place the bottom disc on it, cut side (i.e. crumb) facing up. Using a pastry brush or a tablespoon, soak the bottom disc of sponge with one third of the syrup. Spoon or pipe half of the cream filling over the bottom disc and spread it evenly with the back of a spoon or a spatula.

15. Place the middle disc over the filling, soak it and cover it with the other half of cream. Soak the top layer of sponge with the remaining syrup. Place the top disc over the second layer of filling, taking care when turning it over so that the skin (i.e. the brown side) faces the cream, and the crumb (i.e. the cut side) is exposed on the top of the cake.

16. Using a bread knife, shave off the sides of the cake so the overall shape of the cake is straight and neat. Use a plate or a cake board slightly smaller than the cake laid on the top disc as a guide, if you want to achieve a perfect round shape.

17. Pipe a few spoonfuls of Chantilly cream into a small bowl and use it to crumb-coat the cake with a small spatula. Crumb-coating involves covering the sides and top of the cake with a thin layer of cream to fill any holes or dimples in the crumb structure, and obtain a smooth final coat. The crumb coat is only the foundation to the final coat: at this stage, it is acceptable for the sponge to show through as this will be fully covered with the final coat. Using only the cream in the bowl for crumb-coating avoids spoiling the entire batch with the crumbs that unavoidably stick to the spatula and end up in the cream.

18. Add extra Chantilly cream (this time from the piping bag, not from the bowl) on top of the cake and smooth it down with a small spatula. Finally, use a long spatula, or the straight back of a long bread knife to smooth across the entire top surface and flatten it out with one sweeping movement.

19. If you are writing a message or greeting on the cake with chocolate, this is the time to do it. Should anything go wrong, it is still easy to scrape off the top and start again. It will be much more complicated to do it once the rest of the cake is fully decorated.

20. Pipe vertical strips of Chantilly cream all around the cake sides: move from bottom to top and keep the star nozzle very close to the crumb coat so that the Chantilly sticks well. I recommend this decoration technique as, even though it delivers striking results, the process is rather forgiving. So even those with limited piping skills like me have a very good chance of delivering an elegant cake. Pipe small swirls of Chantilly cream all around the top of the cake: this will help mask any unevenness that may have formed around the top edges of the coating.

21. If you have any leftover cream filling, you can use it to pipe a few extra swirls of cream on the top, which can also be decorated in line with the main flavour of the cake; in this case, whole almonds and dried orange slices, but also pistachios, chocolate buttons, coffee truffles, candied orange peel, hazelnuts, etc… Remember to store the cake in the fridge until it is ready to serve as Chantilly cream is very delicate and it will lose its sharpness if left out of the fridge, especially on a hot day. It can be kept in the fridge for up to 2 days.

ALSO TRY…

You can have fun adding colouring gels to the Chantilly cream: pastel colours are particularly easy to achieve with whipped cream and make a good addition to a kids' birthday cake.

As an easier and egg-free alternative, use more Chantilly cream instead of the pastry cream as a filling: mix in diced fresh or canned (drained) fruit to make a fantastic summery dessert.

ALTERNATIVE FLAVOUR COMBINATIONS

There are several alternatives to the orange and amaretto combination: choose from the list of options below. The syrup should be selected to match the filling's main flavour. Most syrups have an alcoholic and a non-alcoholic option; however, the amount of alcohol is very small and most will have evaporated by the time the cake is ready to eat.

To make any of the syrups, place all liquids (except alcohol, if using) in a small pan, add the sugar and depending on the recipe, citrus peels, vanilla paste or honey. Heat gently, while stirring, until the sugar is dissolved, then remove from the heat and let it cool for a couple of minutes. Finally, add the alcohol, if using, and set aside to cool completely before using.

Amaretto syrup (pages 72–5)

For the milk syrup
180g (¾ cup) water
180g (¾ cup) whole milk
1 tsp clear honey (optional)
80g (scant ½ cup) caster (superfine) sugar

For the fruit juice syrup
330g (generous 1⅓ cups) fruit juice of your choice
110g (scant ⅔ cup) caster (superfine) sugar

For the citrus syrup
330g (generous 1⅓ cups) water
peel of 1 organic lemon
peel of 1 organic orange
1 tsp vanilla bean paste
110g (scant ⅔ cup) caster (superfine) sugar
30–40g (2–3 tbsp) triple sec liqueur (optional)

For the limoncello syrup
300g (1¼ cups + 1 tbsp) water
100g (generous ½ cup) caster (superfine) sugar
60–80g (4–5 tbsp) limoncello liqueur

For the rum syrup
300g (1¼ cups + 1 tbsp) water
100g (generous ½ cup) caster (superfine) sugar
40g (3 tbsp) dark rum

Cream filling	Ingredients and method	Recommended syrups
Vanilla pastry cream	Pages 204–6	Amaretto, milk, fruit, citrus, limoncello, rum
Orange pastry cream	Page 206	Amaretto, milk, fruit, citrus, limoncello, rum
Chocolate pastry cream	Page 206	Amaretto, milk, rum
Coffee pastry cream	Page 206	Milk, rum
Giandula cream	Pages 210–11	Milk, rum
Pistachio cream	Pages 207–8	Amaretto, milk, citrus, rum

CAKES & TARTS

Small & Sweet

Part 2

Canestrelli

MAKES ABOUT 50

3 medium eggs
130g (1⅓ cups) soft wheat 00 flour,
    plus extra for dusting
120g (1¼ cups) cornflour (cornstarch)
150g (scant ⅔ cup) cold unsalted butter, diced
80g (generous ½ cup) icing (confectioners')
    sugar, plus extra to decorate
zest of 1 organic lemon
1 tsp vanilla bean paste
⅛ tsp salt

Canestrelli are a small and delicious biscuit, typical of the Liguria and Piedmont regions. Their texture is simply unique: it is reminiscent of the flakiest shortbread; however, the cunning addition of boiled egg yolk and cornflour to the pastry produces a fine, delicate, almost creamy crumb that literally melts in the mouth.

The secret of *canestrelli* is to take them out of the oven before they start to colour. I recommend baking each tray of biscuits separately, to control their status in the oven more closely for this reason. The technique I have devised to work out when *canestrelli* are ready, is to check their bottoms, rather than being guided by their tops: when the bottoms are lightly golden, they are ready.

Their shape is traditionally that of a six-petal daisy: you can even buy special cutters to mould the pastry. I use a standard biscuit cutter instead and carve the hole in the middle with the tip of a smooth piping nozzle.

Canestrelli are the perfect companion for a tea or coffee, and they make a good gift as they keep fresh for over a week in a sealed container.

1. Place the eggs in a small saucepan, cover with cold water and bring to a simmer over a medium heat. Once the water starts simmering, reduce the heat and boil the eggs for 8 minutes, then drain and set aside to cool.

2. While the eggs cool, place both flours in a large bowl and add the butter. Work the mixture by pinching the pieces of butter with the tips of your fingers to break them into very small lumps, fully coated in flour. Keep working the mixture quickly without crushing it until it resembles fine, loose breadcrumbs.

3. Peel the cold eggs, discard the whites and sieve the yolks by pushing them through the mesh of a strainer with the back of a spoon. Add the sieved yolks, icing sugar, lemon zest, vanilla and salt to the flour and butter mixture. Combine all the ingredients well by scooping the mixture up from the bottom of the bowl and mixing it gently with your fingers without crushing it.

SMALL & SWEET

4. When the ingredients are well combined, start crushing the sandy mixture together. Turn it on to the worktop, fold it over itself and press it down with the palm of your hand a few times until it comes together. The mixture will be very dry and crumbly as there are no liquids in the mix, but only the butter to hold it together. Resist the temptation of overworking it to make it smoother as this will compromise the texture of the biscuits. Work it until it just comes together, wrap the dough in clingfilm and rest it in the fridge for at least 1 hour.

5. Generously dust the worktop with flour and roll the dough to a thickness of 1cm (½in). Use a 4cm (1½in) wide, flower-shaped pastry cutter to cut out the biscuits, then use a 1cm (½in) round cutter to cut out a hole in the middle of each flower. (The tip of a smooth, 1cm/½in diameter piping nozzle is also perfect for the job.) Place the biscuits over a baking sheet lined with baking paper. When this is full, place in the fridge to chill for 20 minutes.

6. While the biscuits chill, place the shelf in the middle of the oven and preheat it to 170°C (340°F/Gas mark 3).

7. Meanwhile, keep shaping the other biscuits with the remaining dough, reworking the offcuts, until you have used all of the dough. Arrange the biscuits on a lined baking sheet.

8. When the first sheet has chilled, bake it for 17 minutes until the biscuits are only just starting to turn golden. *Canestrelli* must not be over-baked or they will acquire a very dry texture. If the edges start to turn amber, they are already over-baked: check the bottoms of the biscuits rather than the tops. When their bottoms are golden, the biscuits are ready. While the first tray bakes, chill the second, ready for the second bake.

9. Move the baked *canestrelli* to a cooling rack. After about 10 minutes, roll them one by one in a bed of icing sugar to coat them thoroughly. You can also dust them with sugar instead, but I prefer brutally dunking them to coat the sides too. Store in an airtight container for up to 2 weeks.

Savoiardi
Lady Fingers

— dairy-free
— nut-free

MAKES 200G (7OZ), 40–50, DEPENDING
ON SIZE

For the batter
110g (3¾oz) egg white (about 3 large egg whites),
    at room temperature
⅛ tsp cream of tartar
⅛ tsp salt
100g (generous ½ cup) caster (superfine) sugar
70g (2½oz) egg yolk (about 4 large egg yolks),
    at room temperature
1 tsp vanilla bean paste
zest of 1 organic lemon
70g (¾ cup) soft wheat 00 flour
20g (¼ cup) cornflour (cornstarch)

To decorate
2 tbsp caster (superfine) sugar, for sprinkling
50g (⅓ cup) icing (confectioners') sugar,
    for dusting

Savoiardi literally means 'from Savoy', as
Piedmont is where this recipe originates from.
Savoiardi are very light, crisp and airy biscuits;
they can be eaten on their own, but their
fat-less structure is ideal for soaking up liquid,
making them the perfect companions for your
morning coffee. Just be careful as they are so
light that they will disintegrate if you hold them
in your beverage for longer than 1–2 seconds.

    Savoiardi are best known and appreciated
as a base for traditional desserts such as
tiramisù (pages 56–8) but they are extremely
versatile as they can be coupled with any
leftover cream filling for a quick layered dessert.

    Savoiardi are rather soft as soon as they
come out of the oven, so it is crucial to leave

them on the cooling rack for the following
24 hours to give them time to develop the
characteristic crispiness in full. After that,
they can be safely stored in an airtight
container for a few days.

    The traditional *savoiardi* recipe does not
include any chemical raising agent, so the
distinctive airiness is whipped in by beating
the egg whites and yolks separately. So,
although the recipe is quite simple, do not
be tempted to cut down on the time required
to incorporate enough air into the batter: this
is essential to achieve the perfect structure.

    This recipe will produce just enough to
make a bowl of tiramisù (pages 56–8).

1. Arrange 2 shelves near the middle of the oven
and preheat it to 170°C fan (375°F/Gas mark 5).
Line 2 baking sheets with baking paper. With
a pencil, draw 3 pairs of lines on each sheet
of paper: these should be aligned to the long
side of the paper and the lines in each pair
should be 8cm (3¼in) apart. These will be used
to help pipe evenly sized biscuits. Reposition
the baking paper on the baking sheets, drawn
side down, and set aside.
2. Place the egg white in the bowl of a stand
mixer fitted with the whisk attachment.
Add the cream of tartar and salt, then mix
at top speed for 1–2 minutes until white and
frothy. With the mixer running, slowly add
50g (¼ cup) of the caster sugar and beat the
mixture for a further 3–4 minutes until it forms
a stiff meringue. You want the meringue to be
as stiff as possible but still creamy. If you over-
beat the whites, they will start looking dry and
almost grainy: if they reach this stage they are

much more difficult to incorporate into the yolks. Set aside.

3. Place the egg yolk in a medium bowl and add the remaining 50g (¼ cup) sugar, the vanilla and lemon zest. Beat the yolk with a handheld electric whisk on the maximum speed for about 10 minutes. The yolk mixture is ready when it is more than tripled in volume and it looks fluffy, stiff and pale.

4. Gently fold one third of the meringue into the yolk mixture, one scoop at a time. Sift both flours into this batter and fold them in very gently until fully incorporated. Pour the batter into the remaining meringue and fold it in until fully combined.

5. Stick the sheets of baking paper to the trays with small smears of batter, then transfer the batter into a piping bag fitted with a 10mm (½in) plain nozzle. Use the lines on the baking paper to pipe 3 rows of 8cm (3¼in) sausages of batter.

6. Sprinkle a little caster sugar over the biscuits, then dust them with a light layer of icing sugar. Wait for 5 minutes, then dust with a second light layer of icing sugar: this will create a sweet, crisp crust over the biscuits and give the *savoiardi* their typical cracked surface.

7. Bake both sheets together for 9–10 minutes, swapping the top and bottom sheet after the first 5 minutes to ensure an even bake. *Savoiardi* are ready when just about golden and when they come off the baking paper easily. I prefer to control the baking more closely by baking the sheets of biscuits individually. In this case, open the door just for 1 second after the first 5 minutes to eliminate the excess moisture. Store in an airtight container for up to 2 weeks.

TIP

I recommend whisking the egg white and yolk separately with a stand mixer and a handheld electric whisk, respectively. This will create more washing up, but it minimises the processing time. If you decide to use the same equipment for both, I suggest you beat the former first, as any residue of yolk in the bowl will make it difficult to whip the egg white into a meringue.

SMALL & SWEET

Amaretti

— gluten-free
— dairy-free

MAKES ABOUT 50

250g (1¾ cups) icing (confectioners') sugar,
  plus extra for dusting
90g (⅔ cup) unblanched whole almonds
10g (¼oz) bitter apricot kernels
⅛ tsp salt
35g (1¼oz) egg white (about 1 medium egg white)
1 tsp vanilla bean paste
¼ tsp natural almond extract

The name *amaretti* comes from *amaro*, literally 'bitter' in Italian, after their unmistakable bittersweet taste. This is due to the addition of small amounts of bitter almonds or apricot kernels to the basic nut and sugar mix.

Amaretti are common all over Italy, albeit with some local variations: in Liguria and in Sardinia they are closer to *paste di mandorla* (page 98) and have a rather soft bite, whereas in Piedmont they are typically dry and crunchy. The recipe below will produce a crispy, partially hollow biscuit, probably the variety most often found in shops and bakeries around the country.

Preparation is exceptionally simple: all you need is a food processor and a clean spray bottle. However, these biscuits are deceptively temperamental: you must follow the steps in the recipe religiously if you want a nicely formed biscuit. Do not be tempted to skip the resting or kneading stages and work quickly when shaping and coating the biscuits before baking; they do not tolerate dwelling...

Because of their complex flavour, amaretti are a perfect companion for coffee, tea and sweet wines like passito or malvasia. They are often used to decorate cakes and tarts or,

crumbled, to top ice cream. Crushed amaretti add a pleasant crunch to creams, like *zabaione* (page 216), and can be used to coat the sides of *deliziose* instead of chopped hazelnuts (pages 141–3). They are the key ingredient and main flavour of *bonèt* (pages 43–4).

Their high sugar content means that they happily absorb moisture from the air and turn soft quickly, but if you store them in an airtight container, you can keep them fresh for over a week.

1. Place 150g (generous 1 cup) of the icing sugar in the bowl of a food processor, add the almonds and apricot kernels, then blitz at high speed for about 40 seconds until the mixture is very fine and floury. Add the remaining 100g (¾ cup) icing sugar and the salt, then blitz again for a further 40 seconds. Add the egg white, vanilla and almond extract, then blitz one final time until the mixture comes together in a smooth, doughy mass. Turn the dough on to a clean and dry worktop, press it down and fold it in half a few times with the help of a scraper. The dough will be quite sticky, so the scraper is essential to help handle it. Wrap the dough in clingfilm and leave it to rest in the fridge overnight.

2. The following day, place the shelf in the middle of the oven and preheat it to 160°C (325°F/Gas mark 3). Line a baking sheet with baking paper.

3. Take the dough out of the fridge, unwrap it (keep the clingfilm) and work it with the pressing and folding action again for a few times. The dough should feel much firmer than the previous day, but the scraper will still be

helpful. Divide the dough into small chunks, about 7g (⅛oz) each. Keeping the size as consistent as possible across the biscuits will ensure an even bake, but if you do not want to weigh the individual biscuits one by one, you can use a teaspoon to make the small portions: 7g (⅛oz) is a bit more than ½ teaspoon.

4. Roll each lump of dough between the palms of your hands to shape it into a small ball, then arrange them on the lined baking sheet, leaving at least 5cm (2in) between them. Form only enough biscuits to fill one baking sheet (about 15), wrap the rest of the dough back in its clingfilm and store it in the fridge until you are ready to prepare another batch.

5. Slightly flatten the top of each ball with your thumb. Use a spray bottle filled with water to spray water on to the biscuits until their surface is completely wet: some droplets will drip down the biscuits and possibly pool on the baking paper. This is perfectly acceptable, and it will not be a problem. Quickly dust the top of the wet biscuits with a thin layer of icing sugar (you will see the sugar disappear when it lands on the wet biscuits) and immediately place the baking sheet in the oven. Bake for 17–18 minutes until the biscuits are a light caramel colour.

6. Remove the biscuits from the oven, slide the baking paper on to a cooling rack and leave the baking tray to cool while you shape the following batch. Take the biscuits off the baking paper only when they are at room temperature. Store in an airtight container for up to 2 weeks.

TIP
Only take the dough out of the fridge when you are ready to shape the biscuits: if the dough warms up or dries out before baking, the amaretti will be misshapen.

ALSO TRY...
The pleasant bitterness of the amaretti depends on the number of apricot kernels added to the dough. I have gone for a 90:10 almonds-to-bitter-kernels ratio to get a subtle, delicate flavour. However, as long as you keep the total amount of nuts to 100g (3½oz), you can fine-tune the bitterness by changing the kernels content to suit your own taste.

Occhi di Bue
Ox Eyes

MAKES 16

For the pastry
370g (1¾ cups) soft wheat 00 flour
120g (1¼ cups) ground almonds
200g (scant 1 cup) unsalted butter,
    diced, cold
150g (generous 1 cup) icing
    (confectioners') sugar
100g (3½oz) egg (about 2 medium eggs), cold
zest of 1 organic lemon
zest of 1 organic orange
1 tsp vanilla bean paste
⅛ tsp salt

For the jam
200g (generous 1 cup) canned apricots, drained
70g (⅓ cup) caster (superfine) sugar
½ tsp pectin
1 tbsp freshly squeezed lemon juice
1 tsp vanilla bean paste

To decorate
icing (confectioners') sugar, for dusting

The shape of *occhi di bue* is very simple and rather common in the baking world: a layer of sweet fruity jam sandwiched between two crumbly biscuits. These were an absolute staple at home when I was growing up. The pastry is a version of *pasta frolla* (page 217) modified to accommodate a generous ratio of ground almonds: I have coupled it here with my favourite jam as I love the way the tanginess of the apricots balances out and complements the sweet fragrance of the almonds. My jam is made with canned apricots, so it can be prepared any time of the year. If you are lucky enough to find a small batch of ripe apricots, you can use the fresh fruit instead, just double the cooking time. And if you want to keep it short and simple, you can also use shop-bought jam!

Occhi di bue are at their best freshly baked, while the biscuits still retain their crunchy, crumbly texture. Over time, the moisture from the jam will soften them up, which I quite like, but if you are after the snap, then you have an excuse to dive into the biscuits straight away.

MAKE THE PASTRY

1. Place the flour and almonds in a large bowl and add the butter. Work the mixture by pinching the pieces of butter with the tips of your fingers to break them into very small lumps, fully coated in flour. Keep working the mixture quickly without crushing it until it resembles fine, loose breadcrumbs.
2. Make a well in the sandy mixture and add the icing sugar, egg, citrus zests, vanilla and salt. Mix the egg and sugar with your hands first, then gradually incorporate the flour mixture by scooping it up from the bottom of the bowl and folding it over, rather than crushing it together: this will create large, well separated flakes of pastry rather than a single homogeneous mass.
3. Turn the dough on to the worktop, flatten it down with the palm of your hands, lift one side with a scraper and fold it in half. Repeat no more than 3–4 times until the dough forms a roughly even mass.
4. Flatten the dough, wrap it in clingfilm and

chill it in the fridge for at least 30 minutes, or ideally for a couple of hours. You can prepare the pastry 1–2 days before baking and store it in the fridge until needed.

MAKE THE JAM

5. Roughly chop the drained apricots and place them in a small saucepan. Add the sugar, pectin, lemon juice and vanilla and bring to the boil, stirring occasionally.

6. Reduce the heat and let the mixture simmer for 3 minutes, then blend it with an stick blender and simmer it for a further 3 minutes. Set aside to cool. Stir the fruit occasionally while simmering, and stir it continuously once blended, as it tends to burn easily.

MAKE THE BISCUITS

7. Place 2 shelves close to the middle of the oven and preheat it to 160°C fan (350°F/Gas mark 4). Line 2 baking sheets with baking paper.

8. Remove the pastry from the fridge, unwrap it and divide it in half. Roll one half to a thickness of 5mm (¼in) on a floured worktop. Use a 7cm (2¾in) round pastry cutter to cut 16 discs of pastry, then remove the offcuts and arrange the discs over a lined baking sheet.

9. Repeat with the other half of pastry to make 16 further discs and arrange them over the second lined baking sheet.

10. Using a 2cm (¾in) round pastry cutter or a collection of shaped pastry cutters roughly the same size, cut out holes from the second batch of discs, in the centre of each biscuit. Set aside the cut-outs for later.

11. Bake both batches of biscuits together

for 13–15 minutes, or until the edges of the biscuits just start to turn golden. After the first 7 minutes, swap the top and bottom sheets to ensure an even bake. Remove from the oven and let the biscuits cool for 5 minutes before taking them off the baking paper and letting them cool completely on a cooling rack.

12. Meanwhile, place the pastry cut-outs on another baking sheet lined with baking paper and bake them in the middle of the oven for 6 minutes. At this stage, you can rework the pastry offcuts into a ball, roll it and cut extra shapes with the small pastry cutters, to bake them in the same tray.

ASSEMBLE

13. Once the biscuits and jam have cooled completely, spread a thin layer of jam over the bottom biscuits (i.e. those without a cut out), and pair each one with a top biscuit.

14. Carefully spoon extra jam into the shaped holes of the top biscuits, spreading the jam evenly with a cocktail stick.

15. Place a biscuit cut-out over each sandwiched biscuit, attaching it with a smear of jam. Decorate the biscuits with a light dusting of icing sugar. Store in an airtight container for up to a week.

ALSO TRY...

You can add a touch of orangey sourness to the biscuits by mixing 1 tablespoon of triple sec liqueur into the cool jam.

Baci di Alassio
Alassio Kisses

— gluten-free
— dairy-free

MAKES 18

For the biscuits
130g (1 cup) blanched hazelnuts
100g (generous ½ cup) caster (superfine) sugar
20g (generous 1 tbsp) unsweetened
    cocoa powder
¼ tsp ground cinnamon
pinch of salt
35g (1¼oz) egg white (about 1 medium egg white)
1 tsp vanilla bean paste
25g (scant 2 tbsp) clear honey

For the filling
70g (2½oz) dairy-free dark chocolate chips
    or bar (50–55% cocoa solids)

These sandwich biscuits are named after Alassio: a beautiful Ligurian town and renowned holiday destination, where they were invented in the early 20th century, allegedly to create a sweet souvenir that the many tourists could bring back home and remember the place by.

These little treats are more than simple biscuits: they are flavoursome, chocolatey and indulgent little pastries made with a generous helping of roasted hazelnuts and cocoa powder. They are delicious on their own but are the perfect match for a cup of hot chocolate. They are naturally gluten-free and, as long as the chocolate is, also dairy-free. The texture is satisfyingly chewy, but they must not be overbaked as they may become very hard very quickly. Some bakers advocate a 12-hour rest of the piped dough in the fridge before baking to create a drier and crispier shell. However, my dad has always used the straight-in-the-oven

approach and it has never failed him: I have tested both methods and, quite frankly, I cannot justify to myself the hassle of having to find the fridge space to chill 2 trays of biscuits.

The trickiest step is undoubtedly piping the stiff dough, so equip yourself with a durable piping bag, a wide enough star nozzle and... a pair of strong hands. Resist the temptation to add extra egg white to loosen the dough as this will result in flat pancakes rather than neatly shaped biscuits. If piping really does not do it for you, then wet your hands and mould the dough into small balls.

The filling can be either plain chocolate or ganache: the latter is smoother and softer as well as more forgiving, as it does not set in minutes. However, given the quantities, filling the biscuits with chocolate might be a better option. Unless you make a double batch, which I strongly suggest: 18 biscuits will disappear in no time and leave you craving more!

MAKE THE BISCUITS

1. Place the shelf in the middle of the oven and preheat it to 180°C fan (400°F/Gas mark 6).
2. Place the hazelnuts in a baking tray and roast for 8 minutes until just about golden. Give the hazelnuts a shake midway through the process to ensure an even bake. Take the hazelnuts out of the oven, let them cool for a few minutes, then chill them in the fridge.
3. Change the oven to the static setting at 180°C (350°F/Gas mark 4).
4. Once the hazelnuts have cooled completely, place them in a food processor, add the sugar and pulse the mixture a few times until fine

and sandy. If your food processor does not have a pulse function, blitz on maximum speed for no more than 10–15 seconds. Avoid over-processing the nuts as they might overheat and leach out oil. Any grittiness due to slightly larger granules of nuts will not be a problem; in fact, it will add to the texture of the biscuits.

5. Transfer the nuts and sugar mixture to a medium bowl, sift in the cocoa, cinnamon and salt, and mix with a spoon until fully combined. Make a well in the centre and add the egg white and vanilla. Incorporate them into the dry ingredients with a spoon to make a stiff paste, then add the honey and combine. The sugar takes a while to dissolve in the liquid ingredients, so stir and fold the mixture for a couple of minutes longer than you think is needed; this will also soften it a little and make piping it easier. Transfer the paste into a piping bag fitted with a 12mm (½in) star nozzle.

6. Piping the biscuits is probably the hardest step, as the mixture is rather stiff. Single-use or silicone piping bags are unsuitable: you should use proper canvas or nylon piping bags for this mixture, or you risk a rupture. For the same reason, if in doubt, use a larger nozzle, as a smaller one will make your life more difficult. Line 2 baking sheets with baking paper and pipe 3–4cm (1¼–1½in) wide dollops, about 3cm (1¼in) apart. You should be able to fit 18–20 biscuits on each tray. Rest the biscuits in the fridge for 12 hours at this stage to develop a slightly crunchier crust, if you have the time and the space; otherwise move to the next step straight away.

7. Bake one tray at a time for no longer than 9–10 minutes. Given the dark colour of the dough, it is pretty difficult to gauge when the biscuits are ready; however, 10 minutes should be more than enough. If in doubt, take them out a minute earlier rather than later: overbaking will make these biscuits tough. Take the biscuits out of the oven and slide the baking paper on to a cooling rack immediately. They will be still soft, so give them a few minutes to cool before taking them off the baking paper.

ASSEMBLE

8. If you are using a chocolate bar, chop it finely with a sharp knife. Place the chopped chocolate or chocolate chips in a small microwave-safe bowl and microwave it for 30 seconds. Take it out and stir the chocolate with a silicone spatula for about 20 seconds to distribute the heat evenly. If there are still bits of solid chocolate, give it bursts of 10 seconds in the microwave, followed by 20 seconds of stirring until all the chocolate is melted. Let the chocolate rest at room temperature for a few minutes to stiffen up. To check whether it is ready, scoop a small amount with the spatula and let it fall back into the bowl: the chocolate is ready when it forms a blob that holds its shape without flowing back into the rest of the chocolate.

9. While the chocolate stiffens up, arrange half of the biscuits upside down on the cooling rack.

10. Transfer the chocolate to a small piping bag with a 3–4mm (⅛in) opening (no nozzle required) and pipe about ½ teaspoon of chocolate on each biscuit. You can also simply spoon dollops of chocolate on to the biscuits using 2 teaspoons. Pair each filled biscuit with its empty counterpart, slightly pressing them together, and place them back on the cooling rack to set. Work quickly or the chocolate will set; I recommend filling a few biscuits, then pairing them immediately rather than filling the whole batch first. Make sure the chocolate has hardened fully before taking the biscuits off the cooling rack. Store in an airtight container for up to a week.

ALSO TRY...

For a softer filling, use a ganache instead of plain chocolate: mix 40g (1½oz) chocolate with 30g (2 tbsp) whipping or double cream, then process them in the microwave as described in step 8. The ganache will take much longer than chocolate to set, so there is no need to rush pairing the biscuits together; in fact, the filling will need 8–10 minutes before it is stiff enough to be sandwiched between the biscuits. Once the biscuits have been filled, they need to rest for 30 minutes–1 hour on the cooling rack to give time for the ganache to fully set.

Paste di Pistacchio
Pistachio Cookies

— gluten-free
— dairy-free

MAKES ABOUT 32

150g (generous 1 cup) whole blanched almonds
180g (1⅓ cups) unsalted pistachio kernels
200g (generous 1 cup) caster (superfine) sugar
70g (2½oz) egg white (about 2 medium
    egg whites), at room temperature
2 tsp clear honey
1 tsp vanilla bean paste
zest of 1 organic orange
icing (confectioners') sugar, for shaping
    and decorating

Paste di pistacchio are a small and delicious variation on the traditional *paste di mandorla* (almond cookies) and are based on a balanced mix of almonds and pistachios. Sicily produces arguably one of the best-quality pistachios in the world, so it is not surprising that this is where these cookies originate from. Nowadays, piles of *paste di mandorla* line the windows of pretty much every single bakery in Italy. They owe their success to the availability of extremely high-quality almonds and to the fact that these cookies hold their freshness for a long time.

    Paste di pistacchio are extremely simple to make, and although I have been respectful of tradition and given them the typical snake-like appearance, they can also be given simpler shapes to shorten the process further.

1. Blitz the almonds, pistachios and caster sugar in a food processor at high speed until the mixture has the texture of coarse sand.
2. Lightly beat the egg white, honey, vanilla and orange zest with a hand whisk or a fork until well combined. Add the ground nuts mixture and combine with a spoon to form a paste. Wrap the paste in clingfilm and chill for at least 1 hour.
3. Meanwhile, set the shelf in the middle of the oven, preheat it to 180°C (350°F/Gas mark 4) and line 2 baking trays with baking paper.
4. Sift a generous layer of icing sugar on to a clean and dry worktop. Roll out the dough into a 5cm (2in) diameter sausage and cut it into discs about 1cm (½in) thick. The dough is rather sticky, so keep it and the worktop dusted with icing sugar at all times to help with handling. Shape each disc into the traditional S shape with slightly pointed ends and arrange the cookies on the prepared baking sheet as you form them.
5. Bake one tray at a time for 10 minutes or until the pointed edges just start to turn amber. The cookies will be very soft when they come out of the oven, so let them cool completely before taking them off the baking paper. Lightly dust the cookies with icing sugar once cold. Store in an airtight container for up to a week.

ALSO TRY...

You can convert this recipe into the more traditional all-almond cookies (*paste di mandorla*) by swapping the 180g (1⅓ cups) pistachio kernels for almonds (making a total of 330g/2½ cups whole blanched almonds) and adding ¼ teaspoon of natural almond extract to the mix.

SMALL & SWEET

Frappe

MAKES ABOUT 40

250g (2½ cups) soft wheat 00 flour, plus extra
   for dusting
100g (3½oz) egg (about 2 medium eggs), at room
   temperature
30g (2 tbsp) unsalted butter, at room
   temperature, diced
30g (2 tbsp) caster (superfine) sugar
2 tbsp sambuca
1 tsp vanilla bean paste
zest of 1 organic lemon
⅛ tsp salt
sunflower or corn oil, for frying
vanilla icing (confectioners') sugar, for dusting

Frappe is one of the many sweets that are
traditionally prepared for Shrove Tuesday,
when Italy celebrates Mardi Gras with a
nationwide carnival. They are simple ribbons
of crispy pastry, deep-fried and covered in
vanilla icing sugar.

Although common across the entire country
(and, in fact, across most of Europe), they are
called different names depending on the region:
crostoli in Veneto, *chiacchiere* in Lazio, *bugie* in
Piedmont, *cenci* in Tuscany, *sfrappole* in Emilia
Romagna... to name just a few. I suppose that
this is just a very small example of how highly
territorial culinary traditions still are across
the nation!

Frappe are a very rustic sweet and are
typically homemade; they should be dusted
with vanilla icing sugar for an irresistible flavour.
The latter is a mix of sugar and vanillin, very
common in Italian baking (it is the same stuff
that coats *pandoro*) and which can be found

easily online, although unflavoured icing sugar
may also be used instead.

The easiest way to prepare *frappe* is by
rolling the pastry very thinly with a pasta maker.
My recipe makes a rather soft dough, which
gives my *frappe* an insuperable crispiness, but
it also means that generous and regular flouring
of surfaces and equipment is critical. If you do
not have a pasta maker, the dough can also be
rolled by hand but achieving an equivalent thin
ribbon with a rolling pin is no easy feat.

The ribbons of pastry are often fried flat,
but my dad has always shaped them with an
interesting twist that I could not possibly do
without. To enjoy *frappe* at their crispiest, eat
them freshly made as soon as they are cool
enough to handle. They are perfectly edible
over the following days, but they may lose some
of their crispiness.

1. Put the flour in a large bowl and make a
   well in the centre. Add the egg, butter, sugar,
   sambuca, vanilla, lemon zest and salt and
   gradually incorporate the flour with your
   hands. When the mixture comes together,
   turn it on to a floured worktop. Work it with
   your hands a little until it becomes smooth,
   then flatten it down into a rectangle. It will be
   rather sticky, but it will become much more
   manageable after chilling. Wrap the pastry in
   clingfilm and chill it in the fridge for at least
   30 minutes.
2. Dust a large, clean and dry worktop with flour.
   Remove the pastry from the fridge, unwrap
   it and divide it into 4 roughly equal pieces.
   Flatten one piece with your fingers, then pass
   it through the rollers of a pasta maker on the

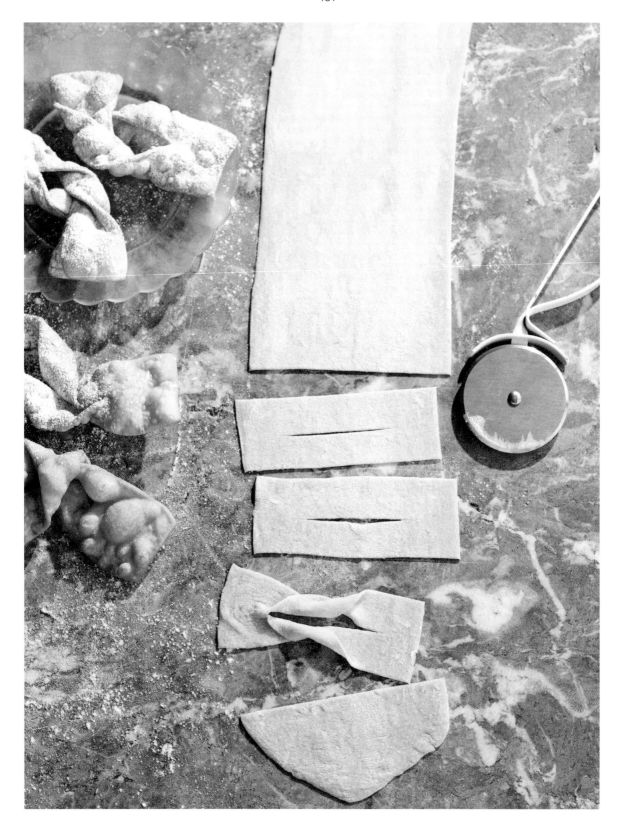

widest setting. Fold the pastry in half, turn it 90° and pass it through the pasta maker on the same setting. Repeat the folding and rolling at least 3 more times. This is needed to refine the texture of the pastry and to make sure that it puffs up in the fryer. Repeat with the remaining pieces of pastry.

3. Now start laminating the pastry to the required thickness: reduce the gap in the pasta maker rollers by one step and pass the pastry through them once more. Work progressively by reducing the gap and rolling the pastry until it is no more than 1.5–2mm (1/16in) thick.

4. Once all the pieces have been processed, you will have 4 strips of pastry, as wide as the pasta-maker rollers (typically 12–15cm/4½–6in). Cut these strips parallel to the shortest side into 4cm (1½in) wide ribbons, using a pizza cutter.

5. Using the pizza cutter, cut a 5cm (2in) slit in the middle of each ribbon, parellel to its longest side. Pass one end of the ribbon through the opening of the slit to create a twist in its 2 long sides. Repeat with all the ribbons.

6. Set the fryer temperature at 180°C (350°F) or use a pan large enough to comfortably fit at least 2 *frappe* and fill it with at least 8–10cm (3¼–4in) of oil. Place it over a medium heat, controlling the temperature with a cooking thermometer. While the oil heats up, line a cooling rack with 2 layers of kitchen paper and place it next to the fryer.

7. When the oil is at temperature, fry 2 *frappe* at a time for about 1 minute per side. *Frappe* will swell significantly when you drop them in hot oil: avoid frying more than 1–2 at a time as you might struggle to turn them over otherwise.

Lift the *frappe* from the oil with a slotted spoon when just about golden and leave to rest on the prepared cooling rack to drain off excess oil. They are overcooked if they reach a caramel or amber colour, and in this case, they are likely to taste bitter.

8. When the *frappe* have cooled to room temperature, place them on a serving plate and decorate with a generous dusting of vanilla icing sugar. They will keep, wrapped in paper, for up to 2 days.

ALSO TRY...

As an alternative to vanilla icing sugar, dust the *frappe* with a blend of 40g (¼ cup) icing (confectioners') sugar and ¼ teaspoon of ground cinnamon.

As an alternative to sambuca, vodka, brandy, whisky or any other liqueur at least 40% alcohol can be used.

Prussiane
Elephant Ears

MAKES ABOUT 18

1.2kg (2lb 10oz) puff pastry (shop-bought
    or homemade, see pages 212–13)
about 200g (1 cup) demerara (light brown) sugar
ground cinnamon, for dusting
1 egg yolk
1 tbsp whole milk

It is not certain why this pastry is named after the long-gone state of Prussia as its origins are still unclear and very much debated. The format, however, is rather common across the baking world, where similar pastries are referred to with different names: *palmiers*, elephant ears, *palmeras* or *orejas*, just to name a few. *Prussiane*, however, tend to be larger and more substantial than other daintier variants.

   The crunchiness of the caramelised sugar coating, perfectly complemented by the flakiness of the pastry, made *prussiane* one of my favourite childhood treats: my dad used to often make them with demerara sugar and an extra dusting of cinnamon for added flavour. I was mesmerised by the way they puffed up in the oven and developed the typical heart shape. This recipe uses a full batch of puff pastry (pages 212–13); however, if prepared with shop-bought pastry, a set of these irresistible yet super-simple treats can be prepared in less than 10 minutes from start to finish. *Prussiane* are ideal to prepare with kids, who I am sure will love observing the shape developing as if by magic in the oven as much as I did.

1. If you are using frozen pastry, take it out of the freezer the day before baking and thaw it overnight in the fridge. Leave it at room temperature for 1 hour before unwrapping it. Avoid unwrapping it when still cold or the condensation on the surface will make it very sticky.

2. Sprinkle a generous handful of sugar over a clean, dry worktop; this will prevent the pastry from sticking to the surface and, at the same time, it will coat the pastry with sugar.

3. Sprinkle some sugar over the top of the pastry too, to stop it from sticking to the rolling pin. Roll the pastry over the sugared surface to a thickness of 1cm (½in), keeping it in a rectangular shape. Shape it so that the side of the rectangle facing you is about 30cm (12in) long. While rolling it, you may need to top up the sugar on the worktop: fold the top half of the pastry over the bottom half and sugar the surface underneath, then repeat for the bottom half.

4. Once the pastry is at your desired thickness, sparingly brush the top with water using a pastry brush, sprinkle a generous amount of sugar over it and dust it with ground cinnamon.

5. Fold the outermost strips (on the left and right edges of the rectangle) towards the centre, and then fold them again so that they almost meet in the centre (see pages 104–105). Fold one rolled-up half over the other to complete the shaping. Cut the rolled pastry in half, wrap each piece in clingfilm and chill in the freezer for 20 minutes. (Scan the QR code for a video tutorial.)

6. Meanwhile, set 2 shelves in the middle of the oven and preheat it to 180°C fan (400°F/Gas mark 6). Line 2 baking trays with baking paper.

A baking tray is preferable to a baking sheet as its edges will stop potential leaks of melted sugar from dripping in the oven. Prepare the egg wash by lightly beating the egg yolk and milk together in a small cup.

7. Take the pastry out of the freezer, unwrap it and cut it into 1.5–2cm (⅝–¾in) thick slices along its length. Place the slices sideways in the baking trays, arranging them at least 5cm (2in) apart as they will puff up while baking. You should be able to fit 6 pastries on each tray, so you may need to bake the lot in 2 batches.

8. Lightly brush the surface of the pastries with the egg wash, sprinkle them with more sugar and bake both trays together for 20–22 minutes or until the pastry is a deep amber colour. After the first 14 minutes, remove the trays from the oven and turn each pastry over with the help of a silicone spatula and a fork, then bake for the remaining 6–8 minutes. Avoid touching the pastries with bare hands when turning them over as they will be coated with very hot, caramelised sugar.

9. Leave the pastries to cool in the tray for 5 minutes before transferring them to a cooling rack. *Prussiane* are best served at room temperature; they should never be stored in the fridge or the pastry will soften up. Store in an airtight container for up to 5 days.

ALSO TRY…
Prussiane are delicious on their own, but they can also be served with *zabaione* (page 216) as a dipping sauce for a more decadent treat.

Scan here to see how to fold puff pastry to make *prussiane.*

— gluten-free
— dairy-free

Ricciarelli

MAKES ABOUT 24

250g (2½ cups) ground almonds or 250g
    (generous 1¾ cups) whole blanched almonds
250g (1¾ cups) icing (confectioners') sugar,
    plus extra for shaping and decorating
zest of 1 organic orange
85g (3oz) egg white (about 2–3 medium egg
    whites), at room temperature
⅛ tsp cream of tartar
1 tsp vanilla bean paste
½ tsp natural almond extract

Nobody visiting Siena could possibly miss the piles of *ricciarelli* proudly stacked on bakery windows. Typically a biscuit baked and given as a present for Christmas, it can now be found all over Tuscany throughout the year. *Ricciarelli* are simple and delicious almond cookies, unmistakably shaped as a rice grain and always coated with a thick layer of icing sugar.

As per most traditional Italian bakes, there are as many variations to the *ricciarelli* recipe as there are families in Siena; nevertheless, one of the best documented mentions of this biscuit in the 19th century stipulates that no flour should be used, making this recipe inherently gluten-free.

The recipe is very simple, but the two slots of resting time are critical to success: chilling the dough overnight will make it more manageable when shaping the biscuits, while leaving the shaped *ricciarelli* to dry before baking ensures the typical cracked surface.

The relatively sticky dough might make shaping fiddly, so I recommend using lots of icing sugar when handling the biscuits to make the job easier.

The biggest mistake when making *ricciarelli* is to over-bake them: the centre of the biscuit should remain soft and gooey, so take them out of the oven as soon as the pointed edges start to become golden.

Traditionally, these biscuits go well with vin santo, coffee or hot chocolate; personally I prefer to cut through their sweetness with a chilled glass of extra-dry prosecco.

1. If using whole almonds, grind them in a food processor following the method on page 13. In a large bowl, mix the ground almonds with the icing sugar and orange zest until fully combined.
2. In a separate bowl, beat the egg whites and cream of tartar with a handheld electric whisk until foamy. Incorporate the vanilla and the almond extract into the egg whites and keep whisking to form stiff peaks.
3. Incorporate the egg whites into the almond mixture to make a paste. You will be knocking most of the air out of the whites while mixing, but this will not be a problem. Wrap the dough in clingfilm and rest in the fridge overnight.
4. The next day, line 2 baking sheets with baking paper and set them aside. Sift a generous layer of icing sugar over a clean, dry worktop and roll out the dough to make a 5cm (2in) diameter sausage. Dust the dough with extra icing sugar to ensure that it does not stick to the worktop.
5. Slice the dough into discs about 12–15mm (½ –⅝in) thick, ensuring that the surface is always generously dusted with icing sugar. Shape each disc into an oval, about 1cm (½in) thick, to give the biscuits the typical rice grain shape. Lay the biscuits over the prepared

baking sheets and dust them again with icing sugar: the surface should be entirely covered in sugar.

6. Let the biscuits rest on the baking sheets for 1–2 hours or until their surface is completely dry. The resting time will depend on the humidity of the room, so check the dryness of the dough by gently pressing on one of the pointed edges: the biscuits are ready to be baked when the dough offers some resistance and cracks when pushed.

7. Meanwhile, set the shelf in the middle of the oven and preheat it to 150°C (325°F/ Gas mark 3).

8. Bake the biscuits, one tray at a time, for 15–16 minutes, increasing the temperature to 180°C (350°F/Gas mark 4) after the first 5 minutes. All being well, the biscuits will crack while baking, creating golden cracks across the white sugared surface.

9. When they come out of the oven, *ricciarelli* are still soft: let them cool completely before taking them off the baking paper. Store in an airtight container for up to a week.

ALSO TRY...
Orange and almond are a flavour marriage made in heaven, so ramping up the orange zest content or using some lemon zest too, although possibly not authentic, works very well.

Ciambelle di Patate
Potato Doughnuts — nut-free

MAKES ABOUT 20

300g (10½oz) floury potatoes, such as Maris
    Piper (about 2 medium potatoes)
50g (3½ tbsp) unsalted butter
300g (2¼ cups) plain (all-purpose) flour,
    plus extra for dusting
2 tsp dry yeast
60g (¼ cup) whole milk
50g (1¾oz) egg (about 1 medium egg)
2 tbsp caster (superfine) sugar, plus 1 extra cup
    for coating
zest of 1 organic lemon
⅛ tsp salt
sunflower or corn oil, for frying

Ciambelle are the Italian equivalent of
doughnuts: the crumb is similarly soft and
sweet, although they are shaped as loops,
rather than rings. In my hometown, they are
traditionally served during the Christmas period:
the slight but unmistakable lemony scent they
exude when dropped in hot oil brings me back
to my grandparents' house at Christmas and
New Year's Eve.

What gives the dough of these *ciambelle*
an inimitable cloud-like texture is the addition
of boiled potatoes. However, for this trick to
work at its best, a couple of precautions must
be taken – ideally, floury potatoes should be
used, I usually go for Maris Piper, and they work
a treat. They must be boiled whole, with their
skins on, to reduce the amount of water they
absorb. Once they are peeled and mashed,
they must be immediately incorporated into
the other ingredients, or wrapped in clingfilm
to avoid forming tough, dry scales on the skin.

Once they are ready to fry, work quickly
through the batch or the last ones will overprove and deflate once fried. These *ciambelle*
do not maintain their freshness for long, so it
is ideal to serve them on the day they are made.
It is only when they are eaten freshly made and
still warm that they perform at their best and
feel as soft and heavenly as candy floss.

1. Place the potatoes in a medium saucepan,
   cover them with boiling water and simmer until
   thoroughly cooked. The timing depends on the
   size, type and freshness of the potatoes, but it
   is likely to be about 30 minutes. The potatoes
   are cooked when you can comfortably push a
   fork through their thickest section.
2. Meanwhile, weigh the butter in a microwave-
   safe bowl and microwave it for 30–40 seconds
   to melt it completely. Stir to make sure that
   there are no solid lumps left and set aside.
3. When the potatoes are cooked, drain the
   hot water and fill the pan with cold water.
   When they are cool enough to handle, peel
   them, place them in a large bowl and mash
   them carefully: the flesh must be reduced
   into a smooth pulp. Pour the butter over the
   mashed potatoes immediately and mix to
   combine. Do not leave the mashed potatoes
   to rest uncovered as they will dry out and
   create flecks that will be difficult to dissolve
   in the dough. Add the flour, yeast, milk, egg,
   2 tablespoons of sugar, lemon zest and salt,
   and mix with your hand to combine.
4. When the dough comes together in a coherent
   mass, turn it on to the worktop and knead
   it for 1–2 minutes until smooth. The dough
   should feel soft, and ever so slightly sticky, but

SMALL & SWEET

not wet. If necessary, add a minimal dusting of flour. Shape the dough into a ball and drop it back in the bowl. Leave it to prove away from cold draughts and direct sunlight until doubled in volume. It should take about 45–50 minutes at 20°C (68°F).

5. While the dough is proving, lay a large, clean dish towel over the worktop and dust it generously with flour. Also lightly flour an area of the worktop ready for shaping the dough.

6. Transfer the proved dough to the floured worktop and divide it into 4 pieces. Work on one piece at a time and progressively roll it into a 1cm (½in) thick noodle. Cut 20cm (8in) lengths, then fold each length to form the characteristic looped shape, pinching the dough to join the ends of the loop where they overlap. Each *ciambella* will be about 35g (1¼oz). Arrange the loops over the floured dish towel as you shape the remaining dough. Cover the loops of dough with a second, clean dish towel and leave them to prove until they look light and slightly swollen. This should take 45–50 minutes at 20°C (68°F). Be careful not to overprove the dough at this stage or the *ciambelle* might deflate once fried.

7. Meanwhile, set the oil temperature in a fryer to 180°C (350°F) or find a pan large enough to comfortably fit at least 3 loops of dough. Fill the pan with at least 8–10cm (3¼–4in) of oil and place it over a medium heat, controlling the temperature with a cooking thermometer. While the oil heats up, line a cooling rack with 2 layers of kitchen paper, and place it next to the fryer. Place a cup of caster sugar in a medium bowl to coat the *ciambelle*.

8. Fry 2–3 *ciambelle* at a time for about 2 minutes, turning them over a couple of times with a slotted spoon to cook them evenly. They are ready when the skin looks a light caramel colour. Rest the fried *ciambelle* over the kitchen paper to drain any excess oil.

9. When the *ciambelle* are cool enough to handle but still warm, toss them in the bowl with the caster sugar to coat them evenly and then move them to a serving plate. Store in an airtight container for up to 2 days.

ALSO TRY...
Swap the milk for a liqueur of your choice, such as limoncello or amaretto, to give *ciambelle di patate* a stronger flavour.

Pasticciotti

MAKES 6

For the cream filling
1 organic lemon
500g (2 cups) whole milk
1 tsp vanilla bean paste
75g (2½oz) egg yolk (about 5 medium egg yolks)
110g (scant ⅔ cup) caster (superfine) sugar
50g (¼ cup) cornflour (cornstarch)
small pinch of salt

For the pastry
250g (2½ cups) soft wheat 00 flour,
    plus extra for dusting
½ tsp baking powder
100g (scant ½ cup) diced lard or unsalted butter,
    at room temperature, plus extra for greasing
100g (generous ½ cup) caster (superfine) sugar
60g (2¼oz) egg (about 1 large egg),
    at room temperature
zest of 1 organic lemon
zest of 1 organic orange
1 tsp vanilla bean paste
pinch of salt
1 egg yolk, for brushing

For the assembly
18 Amarena cherries in syrup, drained

Pasticciotti are mini-cakes made with a crumbly pastry casing and filled with a sweet custard-like cream. One of the most renowned versions originates in the small town of Galatina, in southern Puglia, where they still line the windows of every single bar and bakery. A staple breakfast sweet, today *pasticciotti* are served throughout the day as a substantial treat, as long as they are eaten warm to fully appreciate the fragrance and texture of the rich pastry. The addition of lard is essential to achieve the melt-in-the-mouth crumb; however, this can be swapped for butter if necessary.

Many variations to the basic recipe are available; nevertheless, the only tweak to the simplest version I would recommend is the addition of a few Amarena cherries to the pastry cream, as the added sharpness gives extra depth to the sweetness of the filling.

Pasticciotti are typically baked in individual oval moulds measuring 10 x 6cm (4 x 2½in) and about 2cm (¾in) deep, and must bear the distinctive domed top; however, they can also be baked in small tartlet tins of equivalent size. Avoid muffin trays as the lack of a rim around the base makes it difficult to shape the top.

MAKE THE CREAM FILLING

1. Prepare the cream filling following the method on pages 204–6. The cream filling should be prepared at least 1–2 hours before it is needed to give it time to cool to room temperature before piping it into the pastry cases. It can also be prepared the day before baking and stored in the fridge, lined with clingfilm.

MAKE THE PASTRY

2. Place the flour and baking powder in a large bowl and add the lard. Work the mixture by squeezing the pieces of lard in your hands to break it into very small lumps, fully coated in flour. Keep working the mixture until it resembles fine breadcrumbs.

3. Make a well in the sandy mixture and add the sugar, egg, citrus zests, vanilla and salt. Mix the egg and sugar with your hands first, then gradually incorporate the flour and lard mixture. When the dough comes together, turn it on to a worktop, flatten it with your hands and fold it in half. Repeat the flattening and folding a few times until the dough forms a homogeneous mass. Divide the dough into 2 pieces, one slightly larger than the other, shape them into discs, wrap them in clingfilm and chill in the fridge for at least 30 minutes.

4. Meanwhile, grease and flour the moulds, place the shelf in the middle of the oven and preheat it to 200°C (400°F/Gas mark 6).

ASSEMBLE

5. Flour the worktop and roll the larger pastry disc to a thickness of 5mm (¼in). To make the pastry cases, cut a piece of pastry slightly larger than one mould and, working with your fingers, gently push it into the mould so that it fits snugly. Pinch the pastry against the outside of the mould rim, so that any excess is trimmed off while some pastry is left lining the rim itself. Repeat to line all the moulds, collecting any leftover pastry as it might be needed later to make the lids.

6. Pipe a generous amount of pastry cream into each pastry case, ensuring that it domes above the top edge of the mould: this will give the *pasticciotto* the typical domed shape. Push 3 drained Amarena cherries into the cream dome of each *pasticciotto*.

7. Roll the second pastry disc to a thickness of 5mm (¼in) on the floured worktop, incorporating any pastry offcuts, if needed.

To make the lids, cut a piece of pastry large enough to cover one mould, lay it over the domed cream and, working with your fingers, seal the edges by pinching the pastry against the rim of the mould. Repeat to make lids for all the pastry cases. (Scan the QR code for a video tutorial.)

8. Brush the top of each *pasticciotto* with egg yolk. Place all the moulds into a baking tray and bake for 15–16 minutes or until the tops are a deep golden colour. Store in the fridge for up to 2–3 days.

TIP

The oven temperature must be relatively high to bake the pastry shells quickly while keeping their core temperature low. If the temperature is reduced, the *pasticciotti* will have to be kept in the oven for longer, overcooking the cream, which will likely start to boil, rupturing the shells.

ALSO TRY...

Easy variations to this recipe may include one of the many creams listed in the Basics section (pages 204–11) in combination with fruit jams. For a more decadent version, line the bottom of the pastry cases with a 5–8mm (¼–⅜in) thick layer of almond paste (pages 136–8).

 Scan here to see how to form, fill and shape *pasticciotti*.

Brutti ma Buoni
Ugly but Good

— gluten-free
— dairy-free

MAKES ABOUT 28

100g (3½oz) egg white (about 3 medium egg whites), at room temperature
⅛ tsp cream of tartar
⅛ tsp salt
250g (1⅔ cups) caster (superfine) sugar
300g (2⅓ cups) toasted chopped hazelnuts
½ tsp ground cinnamon

Never was a name more appropriate for a biscuit: *brutti ma buoni* literally translates as 'ugly but good', and that is exactly what these biscuits are: irregular, coarse, knobbly but deliciously sweet and nutty. The origin is debated: some place it in Lombardy, others in Piedmont, although these biscuits have been a classic in Tuscany and Emilia Romagna for a long while. They are certainly a product of northern Italy, understandably, considering that the main ingredient is hazelnuts, of which the North produces loads of very high quality.

Brutti ma buoni are cooked twice: the first time in a pan, the second in the oven. It is much less complicated than it sounds, as long as you take some precautions. First, avoid using a non-stick pan to cook the meringue; go for stainless steel instead. It may sound counterintuitive, but I find that sugar in general tends to stick more to non-stick pans compared to conventional steel. Second, never stop stirring the meringue while cooking, and use a wooden spoon: this will give you a better feeling of what is happening at the bottom of the pan. Third, use the smallest burner you have on the lowest setting; a flame spreader or, even better, a copper pan is ideal to avoid hot spots and therefore burns.

One final point on the hazelnuts: roasting and chopping your own delivers the best result

in terms of taste and crunchiness. However, I tend to use ready-chopped hazelnuts for this recipe, as they are more convenient and guarantee pieces of even size. Ensure that you are using a fresh batch, as chopped hazelnuts can start to taste stale very quickly.

1. To make the meringue, beat the egg whites, cream of tartar and salt in the bowl of a stand mixer fitted with the whisk attachment on medium speed. When the mixture is foamy, increase the speed and add the sugar in 3 batches; the mixture will thicken after each addition. The meringue is ready when glossy, the peaks on the whisk are stiff and do not fold over, and when you can no longer feel the grittiness of the sugar when rubbing it between your fingers. It will take 10–12 minutes.
2. Fold in the hazelnuts and cinnamon with a silicone spatula, then transfer the meringue to a stainless-steel pan. Cook it over a very low heat for 8–10 minutes, stirring continuously with a wooden spoon until it turns amber.
3. Meanwhile, set the shelf in the middle of the oven and preheat it to 140°C (275°F/Gas mark 1). Dampen the worktop with a clean, wet cloth and then turn the mixture on to it. Line a baking sheet with baking paper, fill a glass with water and get a metal spoon ready.
4. Using the metal spoon, take a walnut-sized spoonful of mixture and drop it on to the prepared baking sheet. Dip the spoon in the water and spoon the next dollop of mixture. Repeat until you have used all the mixture.
5. Bake for 25–30 minutes. A longer bake delivers crunchier biscuits, a shorter bake will keep them softer in the centre. Store in an airtight container for up to a week. Delicious served with or crumbled over pistachio ice cream.

Panna Cotta al Marsala
Marsala Panna Cotta

— gluten-free
— egg-free
— nut-free

MAKES 8 POTS, 125ML (4FL OZ) EACH

200g (generous 1 cup) caster (superfine) sugar
7g (⅛oz) platinum grade gelatine leaves
    (about 4 leaves, see page 12)
600g (2⅔ cups) whipping (heavy) cream
    (30–35% fat)
1 tsp vanilla bean paste
2 tbsp white rum
2 tbsp dry Marsala wine

While panna cotta are not technically bakes as they are not cooked in the oven, I could not possibly leave them out of a collection of Italian classics. The name literally means 'cooked cream' as the cream is brought to a simmer with sugar and flavourings before dissolving the soaked gelatine leaves. The origin of this dessert is debated, but most sources agree that it originated somewhere in northern Italy, most likely in Piedmont in the early 20th century.

Compared to older classics, panna cotta is a relatively young addition to the list of Italian desserts, but it has gained popularity rather quickly, both in Italy and abroad, being extremely simple and quick to make. Nevertheless, a couple of precautions must be observed to obtain the all-important silky smooth and flawless texture.

Nowadays, panna cotta is often flavoured only with vanilla and served with a fruit reduction or chocolate sauce, but this version is closer to what was officially recorded in Piedmont in the 20th century: I find that the addition of Marsala wine and rum, as well as the light coating of caramel, creates a much more complex flavour.

Probably, the most difficult step in the making of panna cotta is demoulding it on to the serving plate. Admittedly, the end result looks rather sophisticated, but, if you would rather serve it directly in the individual pots, modify the recipe as detailed in the 'Also try' section (page 120) or check out the *panna cotta soffice al caffè* (page 122), which is set and served in coffee cups.

1. Prepare 8 aluminium pots on a flat, heat-resistant surface (a wooden chopping board is ideal).
2. To make the caramel, melt 100g (generous ½ cup) of the sugar in a small metal saucepan over the lowest heat on your hob. When the edges start melting, tilt and shake the pan to melt all the sugar. At no point in the process should you stir the caramel. The caramel is ready as soon as all the sugar is liquid and deep amber in colour.
3. Carefully pour just enough caramel in each pot to coat the bottom, dividing it evenly. Be very careful at this stage as the caramel is around 200°C (400°F) and can cause serious burns if it gets in contact with the skin. The aluminium pots will get very hot too once the caramel is poured. (Use of protective gloves is recommended.)
4. Soak the gelatine leaves in a bowl of cold water for 10 minutes.
5. Meanwhile, add 300g (1⅓ cups) of the cream, the remaining 100g (generous ½ cup) sugar and the vanilla paste to a small pan and bring to a simmer. By warming up only half of the cream, the cooling/setting time will be shorter, and less alcohol will be lost through evaporation.

SMALL & SWEET

Remove from the heat, squeeze out the excess water from the gelatine leaves and dissolve them in the hot cream, stirring vigorously with a spoon or, even better, a whisk.

6. Very slowly pour the remaining 300g (1⅓ cups) cold cream into the hot cream mixture, stirring constantly. Always add the cold cream into the hot, never the other way around: this will avoid premature setting of the gelatine and the formation of rubbery lumps in the cream.

7. Finally, add the rum and Marsala wine and combine. Divide the mixture equally between the pots; they should be filled up to about 1cm (½in) from the rims. Leave to set in the fridge for at least 3 hours or, better, overnight.

8. Once the mixture is set, demould each pot on to a small plate or saucer. The best way to do this is to fill a bowl big enough to fit one pot with boiling water. Dip each pot in the hot water for no longer than 2–3 seconds, then turn it on to the serving plate. Shake the pot and plate sideways and tap it over a folded dish towel until the panna cotta has dropped. Store in the fridge for up to 2–3 days.

TIP

Do not pour cold water in the hot caramel pan! Set the pan with leftover caramel aside to cool completely. To wash off the caramel from the pan and the pots, fill them with hot water and leave them to soak: the solid caramel will dissolve in the water effortlessly.

ALSO TRY…

My everyday version of panna cotta is served directly in pots or glasses, does not require caramel or demoulding. For a potted panna cotta, reduce the amount of gelatine from 7g to 5g (i.e. use 3 leaves rather than 4) and pour it into fancy glasses (Martini glasses look great). For a non-alcoholic version, omit the rum and Marsala and decorate the top with diced or puréed fruit. Peach, either fresh or canned, goes extremely well with the flavour of Marsala wine.

SMALL & SWEET

Panna Cotta Soffice al Caffè
Soft Coffee Panna Cotta

— gluten-free
— egg-free
— nut-free

MAKES 6 CUPS, 150ML (5FL OZ) EACH

5g (⅛oz) platinum grade gelatine leaves
  (about 3 leaves, see page 12)
600g (2⅔ cups) whipping (heavy) cream
  (30–35% fat)
100g (generous ½ cup) caster (superfine) sugar
1 tsp vanilla bean paste
160g (⅔ cup) espresso
6 tbsp coffee liqueur (optional)

The bitterness of coffee blends particularly well with the sweetness of the cream, so it is no surprise that this flavour combination has rapidly become one of the most common when it comes to panna cotta. My version of coffee panna cotta requires only a minimal amount of gelatine to create an extremely soft and delicate texture, which retains a gentle wobble even after an overnight set. This panna cotta is almost creamy and not suitable to be demoulded, but it should be set and served in coffee cups. Keep it in the fridge until ready to serve, and if using liqueur, only add it just before serving. It is ideal served at the end of a meal instead of coffee and, when combined with elegant cups and saucers, it can be turned into a very sophisticated dessert (yet deceptively simple to make), worthy of the most stylish dinner party.

Ideally, strong espresso should be used in this recipe to convey the all-important coffee flavour; however, coffee made with a stovetop *caffettiera* can be used instead, or even just 4 teaspoons of instant coffee dissolved in 160g (5¾oz) hot water. Needless to say, a good decaf will produce an equally good result.

1. Soak the gelatine leaves in a bowl of cold water for 10 minutes.
2. Meanwhile, add the cream, sugar and vanilla to a small pan and bring to a gentle simmer. Remove from the heat, squeeze out the water from the gelatine leaves and add them to the cream. Stir vigorously with a whisk to dissolve.
3. Add the espresso and combine. Always add the espresso after taking the cream off the heat, or the panna cotta will taste like reheated coffee. Divide the mixture equally between 6 coffee cups and leave to set in the fridge overnight. Covering the cups with clingfilm (or even with their own saucers) will prevent the tops of the panna cotta from forming a skin.
4. Once the mixture is set, pour 1 tablespoon of coffee liqueur into each cup and serve with a saucer and teaspoon. Store in the fridge for up to 2–3 days.

TIP
The minimal amount of gelatine in this recipe demands a rather long setting time, so the panna cotta should be prepared first thing in the morning for an evening with friends, or the day before.

ALSO TRY...
Caffè corretto, i.e. an espresso with a drop of sambuca, is a very popular choice, especially at the end of a generous meal: the aniseed flavour of the liqueur goes particularly well with the bitterness of coffee, so for a dessert with a stronger alcoholic kick, try swapping the coffee liqueur for sambuca. Or, for a more decadent version, go for chocolate liqueur instead.

SMALL & SWEET

Cannoncini
Puff Pastry Cannoli

MAKES 16

400g (14oz) fresh or frozen puff pastry
    (shop-bought or homemade,
    see pages 212–13)
plain (all-purpose) flour, for dusting
1 egg yolk, beaten
2 tbsp granulated sugar
50g (generous ⅓ cup) chopped
    roasted hazelnuts
icing (confectioners') sugar, for dusting

For the cream
400g (1¾ cups) whole milk
1 tsp vanilla bean paste
60g (2¼oz) egg yolk (about 4 egg yolks)
100g (generous ½ cup) caster (superfine) sugar
30g (¼ cup) cornflour (cornstarch)
pinch of salt
40g (1½oz) dark chocolate chips or bar
    (50–55% cocoa solids)
60g (2¼oz) hazelnut butter (shop-bought
    or homemade, see pages 210–11)

Variations of cream horns are ubiquitous across Europe, boasting many formats and flavour combinations. The traditional *cannoncini*, however, are said to originate from early 20th-century Turin and are typically smaller than other European counterparts. Some claim that the early versions were filled with *zabaione*, although today they are more commonly found filled with flavoured versions of *crema pasticcera* (pages 204–6). *Cannoncini* have been unfairly tagged as an old-fashioned dessert; however, in recent years, they have been granted fashionable status again with specialist shops cropping up all over Italy, offering them in a vast array of colours and flavour combinations.

The recipe below uses one third of the batch of homemade puff pastry, although a shop-bought equivalent (chilled or frozen) would be perfectly suitable too. The *gianduia* cream (pages 210–11) makes a perfect companion to the puff pastry and it shares the same roots in Piedmont.

To retain the typical small diameter, mini tube moulds should be used. Those generally sold for Sicilian cannoli have a diameter of about 2.5cm (1in) and are too large for *cannoncini*, which need tubes of less than 1.5cm (⅝in) diameter.

Ideally, *cannoncini* should not be kept in the fridge, as the high humidity compromises the crunchiness of the pastry layers: the filling should be chilled, while the shells should be kept in an airtight container and only filled just before consumption.

1. Make the *gianduia* cream following the method on pages 210–11. This can be made in advance and left in the fridge until needed. The recipe will make more than enough cream to fill all the *cannoncini*.
2. To make the shells, if the puff pastry is frozen, take it out of the freezer the day before baking and thaw it overnight in the fridge. Whether you used chilled or thawed puff pastry, leave it at room temperature for 1 hour before unwrapping it. Avoid unwrapping it when still cold or the condensation will make it very sticky. This applies to both homemade and shop-bought pastry.

3. Set the shelf in the middle of the oven and preheat it to 190°C (375°F/Gas mark 5). Line 2 baking trays with baking paper.
4. Generously flour a worktop and roll out the puff pastry into a rectangle, 3mm (⅛in) thick and with long sides of 35cm (14in). Try to keep the rectangular shape as regular as possible while rolling the pastry.
5. Using a rigid ruler and a pizza cutter, slice the rectangle parallel to the short side, into 16 strips of pastry, each 2cm (¾in) wide. If you use a knife, cut the pastry with a guillotine motion and avoid dragging the blade, as the pastry is very soft and deforms easily. Prepare the beaten egg yolk and a pastry brush nearby. Wind each strip of pastry around one tube mould, slightly overlapping and gently pressing the spirals together. Seal the final spiral in place with a small dab of egg yolk: this will stop the strip unwinding when it puffs up in the oven.
6. Arrange the shells on the baking trays at least 5cm (2in) apart, as they will puff up while baking. Gently brush the top of each shell with the remaining beaten egg yolk and sprinkle over the granulated sugar. Bake one tray at a time for 18–20 minutes or until the top of the pastry is a deep amber colour. Let the shells cool completely before extracting the moulds. The baked shells can be stored in an airtight container for up to 5 days.
7. When you are ready to fill the shells, transfer the *gianduia* cream into a piping bag fitted with a small, plain nozzle, about 8mm (⅜in) diameter. Alternatively, if you are using a disposable piping bag, you can avoid using a nozzle altogether and just cut the tip of the bag to make an 8mm (⅜in) opening.
8. Pipe the cream into the shells from one side until the filling just about bulges out of the opening. Repeat on the other side so each shell is entirely filled with cream.
9. Place the chopped hazelnuts in a bowl and dip both ends of each *cannoncino* into it, so the nuts completely coat the cream. Arrange on a serving plate and decorate with a light dusting of icing sugar. Store in the fridge for up to 2 days.

ALSO TRY...
If you are not a fan of chocolate, you can use conventional *crema pasticcera* (pages 204–6) or flavour it with orange or coffee (page 206) instead of the *gianduia* cream or even go back to basics and fill them with *zabaione* (page 216). In the latter case, use 40g (scant 3 tbsp) Marsala instead of 80g (⅓ cup) and leave the *zabaione* to chill in the fridge overnight to ensure that it develops the necessary thickness to be piped into the *cannoncini* without leaking out.

Zeppole di San Giuseppe
Saint Joseph's Pastries

— nut-free

MAKES 12

For the pastry cream
1kg (4 cups) whole milk
2 tsp vanilla bean paste
1 organic lemon
150g (5½oz) egg yolk (about 10 medium
    egg yolks)
220g (1¼ cups) caster (superfine) sugar
100g (1 cup) cornflour (cornstarch)
pinch of salt

For the choux rings
100g (scant ½ cup) water
200g (scant 1 cup) whole milk
120g (generous ½ cup) unsalted
    butter, diced
⅛ tsp salt
1 tsp caster (superfine) sugar
140g (scant 1½ cups) soft wheat 00 flour
40g (¼ cup) strong bread flour
340g (11¾oz) egg (about 6 medium eggs)
sunflower or corn oil, for frying

For the assembly
12 Amarena cherries in syrup
icing (confectioners') sugar, for dusting

In Italy, Saint Joseph's Day on 19 March is also Father's Day. In most regions of the southern country, this is celebrated with *Zeppole di San Giuseppe*, a substantial beignet, filled with pastry cream and decorated with syruped Amarena cherries.

The concurrence of the two celebrations and the fact that Giuseppe is the most common male name in Italy means that pretty much every family will have an excuse for serving these delicious pastries on the day. And invariably, in every family the never-ending debate will kick off as to whether they should be fried or baked... Although my preference is for the latter version, the recipe below will make a choux suitable for both: the method is based on the fried option, but the 'Also try' section details how to bake them.

MAKE THE PASTRY CREAM

1. Prepare the pastry cream following the method on pages 204–6. If you prepare the cream in advance, store it in the fridge, in a piping bag fitted with a 10mm (½in) star nozzle, holding the tip and back sealed with plastic clips, so it is ready when you want to fill the pastries.

MAKE THE CHOUX RINGS

2. Prepare the paper supports for the choux rings by cutting 12 squares of baking paper, each about 12cm (4½in). Draw a 5cm (2in) diameter circle in the centre of each paper square with a pencil and set aside.
3. Pour the water and milk into a small saucepan and add the butter, salt and sugar, then slowly bring the mixture to a gentle simmer to melt the butter. The pan should be heated very slowly so that the butter melts before the mixture starts to simmer. When the milk mixture starts to simmer, remove from the heat and add both flours in one go, no need to sift them. Mix quickly using a wooden spoon to make a paste.

4. Return the pan to a medium heat and cook the paste while mixing it with the wooden spoon: you want to dry out the mixture by releasing as much steam as possible. The paste is ready when a thin film coats the bottom of the steel pan, or after about 8–10 minutes.

5. Transfer the paste to the bowl of a stand mixer fitted with the paddle attachment and mix on low speed for 5–8 minutes to cool it down.

6. Meanwhile, weigh the eggs into a spouted jug. Then set the mixer speed to medium-high and start pouring roughly one egg at a time into the bowl, making sure that each addition is fully incorporated before adding more. Scrape the sides of the bowl with a silicone spatula, if needed. The appearance of the batter will change from dull and lumpy to smooth and shiny.

7. Check the batter before adding the last egg, which should be used only if the batter is still too stiff and dry. If the batter is already at the right consistency, the last egg might not be needed. The batter is ready when it appears creamy but still stiff. The typical way of checking this is to scoop up a bit of batter with a spatula and then let it drop back in the bowl; if the batter left on the spatula forms a V shape, then it is ready. My favourite method for checking the readiness of the batter, however, consists of pinching then releasing a small amount of batter between my thumb and index finger: if the tip of the batter resting on the bottom finger stays straight up after pinching it, then the batter is still too stiff, and it needs more egg. If just the very tip of the batter slightly tilts after pinching it, then it is already at the perfect consistency and it does not need any more egg.

8. When the batter is ready, transfer it to a piping bag fitted with a 15mm (⅝in) star nozzle.

9. Set the fryer temperature at 180°C (350°F) or use a pan large enough to comfortably fit at least one paper square and fill it with at least 8–10cm (3¼–4in) of oil. Place it over a medium heat, controlling the temperature with a cooking thermometer. Line a cooling rack with 2 layers of kitchen paper and place it next to the fryer.

10. Pipe a ring of batter on each baking paper square, following the drawn circle with the tip of the nozzle as a guide. This will make rings with a diameter of about 8cm (3¼in). The pencil used to draw the circles will transfer to the pastry if you pipe it directly over it; to avoid this, ensure that the drawn side of the paper is facing down and that you pipe the batter on the opposite side. If the nozzle leaves an unsightly spike of choux after piping the ring, flatten it out gently with a wet finger.

11. Gently drop one ring at a time in the hot oil, paper side up, laying it down away from you. After a few seconds, remove the paper with silicone tongs and fry the ring for 3 minutes. Then turn it over, so the top side faces up, and fry it for a further 3 minutes. Finally, turn it upside down again, and fry it for a final minute. Each ring will fry for about 7 minutes until it is a deep amber colour all over. Lift the ring from the oil with a slotted spoon and rest it on the lined cooling rack to drain any excess oil.

12. Fry all the pastries and leave them to cool completely on the cooling rack. Store in an airtight container for up to a day.

ASSEMBLE

13. Slice each pastry open with a bread knife, as if slicing a bun to prepare a sandwich. Pipe a ring of cream in the bottom half of a pastry. Close it with the top half and pipe a small swirl of cream in the centre of the ring. Top the cream with an Amarena cherry and repeat until all the pastries are filled.
14. Finally, decorate the lot with a generous dusting of icing sugar. Store in the fridge for up to 2 days.

TIP

Avoid non-stick pans for cooking the choux paste and, if possible, use a stainless-steel pan. When the paste is ready, it will coat the bottom of a steel pan, but this will not work on a non-stick coating.

ALSO TRY... BAKED ZEPPOLE

For the baked version of *zeppole*, you will not need to prepare the baking paper squares in step 1. Instead, line 2 baking sheets with baking paper and draw six 5cm (2in) diameter rings on each sheet of paper, at least 10cm (5in) apart.

In step 9, rather than heating the oil, place the shelf in the middle of the oven and preheat it to 180°C (350°F/Gas mark 4). Bake one tray of pastries at a time for 30–32 minutes, briefly opening the oven door after the first 10 minutes to let the moisture out. The pastry shells are ready when they are light brown all over with light golden cracks on the surface. If the cracks are pale, it means that the inside of the shells is still raw and moist: if you take the beignets out of the oven at this stage, they might deflate. Store in an airtight container for up to a week (unfilled).

Although traditional *zeppole* are filled exclusively with pastry cream and topped with Amarena cherries, this method can be used to make beignets filled with whatever cream you fancy: a filling of *gianduia* cream (pages 210–11) topped with a few whole hazelnuts or a filling of pistachio cream (pages 207–8) topped with almonds are just a couple of inviting combinations that you can try.

Maritozzi

MAKES 8

For the preferment
50g (generous 3 tbsp) lukewarm water
2 tsp clear honey
2 tsp dry yeast
50g (⅓ cup) strong bread flour

For the dough
40g (¼ cup) sultanas (golden raisins)
200g (scant 1½ cups) strong bread flour
50g (¼ cup) caster (superfine) sugar
50g (generous 3 tbsp) whole milk
60g (2¼oz) egg (about 1 large egg),
    at room temperature
zest of 1 organic orange
1 tsp vanilla bean paste
2 tbsp extra virgin olive oil
⅛ tsp salt
30g (2 tbsp) pine nut kernels
1 egg yolk, for brushing
1 tbsp whole milk, for brushing

For the filling
200g (scant 1 cup) whipping (heavy) cream
    (35–40% fat), cold
30g (2 tbsp) icing (confectioners') sugar,
    plus extra for dusting
1 tsp vanilla bean paste
slivers of fresh fruit, to decorate (optional)

Maritozzi are the Mediterranean equivalent of brioche bread buns, and, in true Mediterranean style, they are made with extra virgin olive oil rather than butter. They are quintessentially Roman, and some historians claim that the recipe is the direct descendant of an old form of bread, usually sweetened with honey and raisins, common in historic Rome centuries ago.

The name is a funny take on the word *marito*, or husband, as it seems that *maritozzi* used to be gifted to the bride-to-be by their fiancé, and occasionally used to hide a small jewel as a present. Nowadays, *maritozzi* are a much more mundane breakfast bun, ubiquitous in Roman bars and bakeries, but rather common throughout the entire Lazio and Marche in central Italy. It is surprisingly versatile, in that it can be served with or without the cream filling, with a plain dough or enriched with candied citrus peel, raisins, pine nuts or even with small chocolate chips.

The making requires relatively long proving slots, but it is rather simple and does not require any special skills other than patience: the result, on the other hand, is absolutely eye-catching and incredibly mouth-watering.

MAKE THE PREFERMENT

1. Pour the water into a medium bowl, add the honey and mix well with a silicone spatula until the honey is fully dissolved. Add the yeast and stir the mixture until the yeast is fully dissolved too. Add the flour and combine with a silicone spatula to make a smooth paste. Clean the sides of the bowl well with the spatula and gather the paste at the bottom of the bowl: any leftover on the sides of the bowl is likely to dry out and form flecks of hard dough that will be difficult to dissolve later.
2. Cover the bowl with clingfilm and leave to prove, away from cold draughts and direct sunlight, until doubled in volume at room

temperature. The oven is the ideal place to prove the preferment. This should take about 1 hour at 20°C (68°F). The preferment is ready when small bubbles are visible on its surface.

MAKE THE DOUGH

3. Meanwhile, place the sultanas in a small bowl, cover with boiling water and set aside to soak.
4. Place the flour in the bowl of a stand mixer fitted with the dough hook. Add the sugar, milk, egg, orange zest, vanilla, oil and the proved preferment. Start mixing on medium speed. When the dough comes together evenly, sprinkle in the salt and continue mixing on medium-high speed for about 15 minutes until the dough wraps around the hook and comes cleanly off the sides of the bowl. Take the dough out of the bowl and roughly stretch it over a clean, dry worktop.
5. Drain the sultanas, squeeze out any excess water, and sprinkle them over half of the dough. Sprinkle the pine nuts over the same side. Fold the side without filling over the other side of the dough and press down with the palm of your hands to incorporate the filling. Repeat the folding and pressing a few times until the filling is evenly distributed within the dough. The dough is very sticky at this point, so you will need a scraper to help you lift it off the worktop. You can also add the filling directly to the bowl of the mixer and let the machine incorporate it into the dough. This looks like a quicker method, but it is not as effective at distributing the filling as the manual route, and it often leads to squashed sultanas and broken pine nuts. Transfer the dough into a large, oiled bowl, cover it with clingfilm and leave it to prove until doubled in volume. This should take about 3 hours at 20°C (68°F).

SHAPE THE DOUGH AND BAKE

6. Meanwhile, line a baking sheet with baking paper and set aside.
7. Drop the proved dough on to a clean and dry worktop. Cut the dough in half with a knife or a scraper, then halve each part twice more until you get 8 equal chunks, about 60g (2¼oz) each. Work the pieces of dough one at a time: while holding a piece with your fingers, gently stretch it and fold it in half over itself a few times, then shape it into a ball and seal the bottom by pinching it firmly. Place the shaped dough on the prepared baking sheet, sealed side down, and repeat for all the dough. If you find the dough too sticky to handle, wet your hands with a few drops of water.
8. Cover the tray with clingfilm or place it in a clean proving bag, and let the dough prove once more until doubled in volume. This should take about 1½ hours at 20°C (68°F).
9. When the dough is almost ready, place the shelf in the middle of the oven and preheat it to 180°C (350°F/Gas mark 4).
10. Beat the egg yolk with the milk and delicately brush it over the top of each *maritozzo* with a pastry brush. Bake for 17–18 minutes or until the top is a deep amber colour, then take the tray out of the oven and let the *maritozzi* cool to room temperature. Store in an airtight container for up to 2 days or freeze for up to a month.

MAKE THE FILLING AND ASSEMBLE

11. While the *maritozzi* cool, pour the cold cream into a metal bowl, add the sugar and vanilla and start whisking on low speed with a handheld electric whisk to combine. Increase to high speed and keep whisking until the cream starts to thicken and the whisk leaves visible marks in the cream. Reduce the speed to medium and as soon as the cream goes from shiny to completely dull, stop whisking. This should take about 2–3 minutes. Spoon the cream into a piping bag fitted with a 10mm (½in) plain nozzle, seal the back and the tip of the piping bag with plastic clips and keep it in the fridge until ready to use. If using a disposable piping bag, no nozzle is necessary: leave the tip sealed until needed and cut it off just before piping.

12. Once the *maritozzi* are at room temperature, cut a deep slit in the top, at a 45° angle, stopping 5mm (¼in) from the bottom: you want the slit to go almost all the way through the bun, without cutting it in two. Hold the slit wide open with one hand and with the other fill the opening with a generous amount of whipped cream. Ensure that the bun is at room temperature throughout before piping in the filling, as a warm crumb will melt the cream. Smooth the top of the cream across the open slit with a spatula or a knife.

13. Arrange the buns on a serving plate and very lightly dust with icing sugar. Decorate with slivers or slices of fresh fruit, if you like. Store in the fridge for up to a day.

ALSO TRY…

I like to decorate the 'smile' of whipped cream with pieces of fresh fruit, but you can also sprinkle it with chocolate shavings, chopped nuts or hundreds and thousands.

I strongly recommend enjoying *maritozzi* the way Romans do in the summer: swapping the whipped cream for a generous scoop of gelato. You will thank me later!

Minne di Sant'Agata
Saint Agatha's Breasts

MAKES 12

For the almond paste
270g (2 cups) whole blanched almonds
60g (4 tbsp) water
270g (1½ cups) caster (superfine) sugar
1½ tsp clear honey
1 tsp vanilla bean paste
¼ tsp green food colouring gel
icing (confectioners') sugar, for dusting

For the pan di Spagna
100g (3½oz) egg (about 2 medium eggs),
    at room temperature
60g (⅓ cup) caster (superfine) sugar
½ tsp vanilla bean paste
zest of 1 organic lemon
pinch of salt
butter, for greasing
40g (generous ⅓ cup) soft wheat 00 flour
30g (2 tbsp) cornflour (cornstarch)
icing (confectioners') sugar, for dusting

For the filling
700g (1lb 9oz) ricotta, preferably sheep's milk
140g (¾ cup) caster (superfine) sugar
2 tsp vanilla bean paste
110g (3¾oz) small dark chocolate chips
    (50–55% cocoa solids), small enough to
    pass through a 15mm (⅝in) nozzle

For the assembly
50g (1¾oz) pasteurised egg white
250g (1¾ cups) icing (confectioners') sugar
1 tbsp freshly squeezed lemon juice
¼ tsp natural almond extract
about 2 tbsp water
12 red candied cherries

Saint Agatha is the patron saint of Catania: the festivity in February is warmly anticipated by the locals and always celebrated, amongst many traditions, with *minne di Sant'Agata*. It is not just the shape of these pastries that blatantly alludes to womanly physical features, as *minne* (or *minni*) literally means breasts in the local dialect.

There are a couple of different theories about the origins of this pastry, one referring to the martyrdom of the saint, another to even older pagan rituals: either way, the shape is only apparently cheeky, and it appears to be, in reality, drenched with deep references to fertility and respect for feminine virtues.

These delicate pastries have a core of ricotta cream over a soft *pan di Spagna* base, topped with a layer of sweet almond paste and coated in royal icing. They are shaped in half-sphere, 7cm (2¾in) diameter, silicone moulds. In principle, these small cakes could also be made in silicone muffin moulds, but the quantities ought to be adjusted as they tend to be smaller.

As with many ricotta-based sweets, ideally sheep's milk ricotta should be used, but where this is not available, conventional cow's milk ricotta can be substituted instead. As in the recipe for *cannoli*, artisanal ricotta is best sieved to give it a creamy consistency, whereas commercial grades can simply be creamed with a handheld electric whisk.

The original recipe requires soaking the sponge base with *rosolio*, a local liqueur, but I prefer not to do this as it makes it really unstable and difficult to transfer to the serving plate undamaged. However, amaretto or maraschino are good options for those who really want an alcoholic version.

Historically, the icing has always been made with unpasteurised egg whites; however, this might expose consumers to health risks, so I usually go for a carton of pasteurised eggs, especially if the kids are having some.

1. The day before making *minne di Sant'Agata*, place the ricotta in a sieve over a bowl, and keep it in the fridge overnight to drain off any excess liquid.

MAKE THE ALMOND PASTE

2. Place the almonds in a food processor and blitz them on full speed until they look like fine sand, but for no longer than 30–40 seconds or they may start leaching oil. Place the water and sugar (in this order) in a medium saucepan and bring it to a simmer over a medium heat to dissolve the sugar. Do not disturb the syrup while simmering: this will minimise the possibility of the sugar crystallising. Once the sugar is fully dissolved, remove the pan from the heat, wait until it cools a little, then add the honey, vanilla, food colouring gel and mix. Add the ground almonds in 3 stages and mix with a wooden spoon until the resulting paste comes cleanly off the sides.
3. Lightly wet a clean worktop and drop the warm paste on to it. Press the paste down with the palm of your hand and, with the help of a wet scraper, lift one side and fold it over the rest. Repeat the pressing and folding action a few times to refine the texture of the paste, then wrap it in clingfilm and chill in the fridge for at least 30 minutes.

MAKE THE PAN DI SPAGNA

4. Set the shelf in the middle of the oven and preheat it to 180°C (350°F/Gas mark 4).
5. Place the eggs in the bowl of a stand mixer fitted with the whisk attachment, add the sugar, vanilla, lemon zest and salt, then whisk at maximum speed for at least 5–7 minutes until the mixture has tripled in volume and looks pale, foamy and rather stiff.
6. Meanwhile, grease and line a 25 x 40cm (10 x 16in) Swiss roll tin, making sure that the sheet of baking paper is large enough to cover the sides too.
7. Sift both flours into the whipped egg mixture in 3 stages and fold in each addition very gently by hand using a silicone spatula until just incorporated. I find that a handheld flour sifter is an ideal tool for this job. Do not overmix to avoid deflating the batter; however, make sure that no lumps of flour are left. When folding the batter, make sure to scrape the bottom of the bowl, which is where the flour very often clump up.
8. Immediately pour the batter into the tin and level off the surface as accurately as possible with an offset spatula. Do not shake or tap the tin to avoid knocking the air out of the batter. Bake for 13 minutes until the sponge feels springy to the touch and the edges look slightly detached from the sides of the tin.
9. While the sponge bakes, prepare a sheet of baking paper, larger than the tin, on a cooling rack and dust it generously with icing sugar. As soon as the sponge comes out of the oven, turn it over the prepared sheet of baking paper, carefully lift the hot baking tin off, then peel off the paper the sponge was baked in.

The sponge will be about 1cm (½in) thick. Cover the sponge with a clean dish towel and let it cool on the cooling rack.

10. Once the sponge is at room temperature, slide it over the worktop and, with a round, 7cm (2¾in) biscuit cutter, cut out 12 discs.

MAKE THE FILLING

11. Once drained, shop-bought ricotta can be used as is, artisanal sheep's milk ricotta will need sieving. This can be done by pushing it through the mesh of a strainer with the back of a spoon. Place the ricotta in a large bowl and whisk it with a handheld electric whisk until creamy. Add the sugar and vanilla and whisk again to combine. Add the chocolate chips and fold them in by hand. Transfer the cream into a piping bag with a plain 15mm (⅝in) diameter nozzle. Pinch the tip and the back of the bag closed with plastic clips and store it in the fridge until needed.

ASSEMBLE

12. Coat the inside of the moulds with a generous dusting of icing sugar. Dust a clean, dry worktop with a generous layer of icing sugar and roll the almond paste to a thickness of 3mm (⅛in). *Pasta di mandorle* has a high humidity content and soaks up the icing sugar very quickly, so re-dust the surface generously and often to make sure that it does not stick. Use a 12cm (4½in) diameter pastry cutter to cut out 12 discs of the paste. You will likely need to gather offcuts and roll them again to obtain 12 discs, however, this is easy to do as *pasta di mandorle* is

very resilient and it will not suffer from being reworked over and over again. If it is a very warm day, however, it is advisable to chill it in the fridge for 10 minutes before reworking it, to stop the nuts from leaching out oil.

13. Line each half-sphere mould with a disc of *pasta di mandorle*: if this breaks in the process, just press the broken bits together again. Any folds created while shaping the paste into the mould can be pressed down too. This step is rather fiddly; however, the layer of *pasta di mandorle* does not need to be perfect as long as it is of a reasonably consistent thickness and it lines the whole mould, leaving no parts exposed. The icing coating will mask any cracks or imperfections, but if the creamy filling gets to the mould, it will make it difficult to release the domes. Trim off the excess *pasta di mandorle* by sliding a knife over the rim of each mould.

14. Pipe the ricotta cream into each mould, filling it all the way up to the top. Level off with a spatula or a knife, if necessary. Top each mould with a disc of *pan di Spagna* and transfer to the fridge to chill for at least 1 hour.

15. While the domes are chilling, prepare the royal icing: place the egg white and the icing sugar in the bowl of a stand mixer fitted with the whisk attachment, add the lemon juice and whisk on low speed to combine. Then ramp up to full speed and whisk for about 5 minutes until the mixture is smooth, glossy and stark white. Add the almond extract and whisk to incorporate. The resulting mixture is very thick, almost like a paste: you will need to add a couple of tablespoons of water to thin it down to a pourable consistency. To ensure that you are adding the right amount of water,

add 1 tablespoon at a time, fold it in with a silicone spatula, then check the texture. The texture is right when the mixture flows off the spatula in a continuous ribbon and it leaves a trail on the icing in the bowl that disappears in a few seconds. Fold the water in with a spatula and avoid whisking it in with the mixer as this would incorporate a lot of air bubbles and spoil the appearance of your coating.

16. Turn the chilled domes over a cooling rack and place this over a roasting tray. Ease them out by tapping the cooling rack on the worktop or gently pulling the silicone of the mould. Avoid pushing them out by pressing on the back of the moulds as the filling is very soft and you would inevitably deform the domes.

17. Using a spoon, pour royal icing over the domes, coating them one by one. Spread the icing around the dome very gently using the back of the spoon to make sure that the entire surface is coated. You should need just over 1 heaped tablespoon of icing per dome. Place a cherry on each dome before the icing sets. The tray at the bottom of the cooling rack will capture any excess icing. Wait until the domes do not drip any more icing, then lift them up gently with a spatula and move them on to individual saucers or small cardboard discs. Cool them in the fridge for at least 30 minutes to set the icing before serving. Store in the fridge for up to 2–3 days.

ALSO TRY...

Recycle *pasta di mandorle* leftovers by rolling them into little balls and coating them with melted dark chocolate. They make the perfect *pasticcini* for an afternoon tea!

Deliziose

MAKES 12

For the *pasta frolla* pastry
400g (4 cups) soft wheat 00 flour, plus
    extra for dusting
200g (scant 1 cup) unsalted butter, cold
140g (1 cup) icing (confectioners') sugar
100g (3½oz) egg (about 2 medium eggs), cold
zest of 1 organic lemon
1 tsp vanilla bean paste
⅛ tsp salt

For the filling
50g (1¾oz) dark chocolate chips or bar
    (50–55% cocoa solids)
400g (1¾ cups) ricotta
50g (¼ cup) caster (superfine) sugar
zest of 1 organic orange
¼ tsp ground cinnamon

For the assembly
60g (scant ½ cup) roasted chopped hazelnuts
icing (confectioners') sugar, for dusting

Deliziose literally means 'delicious' in Italian,
and no other name would better describe these
unpretentious and super-easy sandwich biscuits.
The biscuits are simple discs of *pasta frolla*
(page 217) and the filling also requires minimal
preparation. Despite their simplicity, *deliziose*
truly live up to their name and have for a long time
been an unmissable addition to the traditional tray
of pastries that is served at the end of a Sunday
meal in central and southern Italy.

    Needless to say, the versions of this
dessert are endless, but the most straightforward
ricotta filling is my favourite. Over time, the

moisture from the filling will creep into the
pasta frolla, so after a day or so of resting
the sandwich acquires a soft, creamy bite.
If you would rather keep the biscuits crunchy,
assemble the *deliziose* just before serving them.

    Deliziose must be stored in the fridge and
consumed within a couple of days because of
the high ratio of fresh cheese in the filling. In
all honesty, I would be surprised if they lasted
that long!

MAKE THE PASTRY

1. Prepare the *pasta frolla* following the method
on page 217. *Pasta frolla* can be prepared up
to a couple of days in advance and stored
wrapped in clingfilm in the fridge until needed.

MAKE THE FILLING

2. If you are using a chocolate bar, grate it with
a box grater. If you are using chocolate chips,
chop them finely with a sharp knife and place in
a medium bowl. Add the ricotta, sugar, orange
zest and cinnamon to the bowl and mix with a
handheld electric whisk until smooth.

3. If you intend to pipe the filling on to the
biscuits, transfer it to a piping bag with a
10mm (½in) smooth nozzle. Pinch the tip and
back of the bag with plastic clips and store
in the fridge until needed. If you are spooning
it on, cover the bowl with clingfilm and keep
it in the fridge until needed.

BAKE AND ASSEMBLE

4. Place 2 shelves close to the middle of the oven and preheat it to 160°C fan (350°F/ Gas mark 4). Line 2 baking sheets with baking paper.
5. Work on one half of the pastry at a time: remove it from the fridge and roll it over a floured worktop to a thickness of 5mm (¼in). Use a 7cm (2¾in) pastry cutter to cut 12 discs of pastry, remove the offcuts and arrange the discs over a lined baking sheet.
6. Repeat with the other half of pastry to make 12 further discs and arrange them over the second lined baking sheet.
7. Bake both batches of biscuits together for 11–12 minutes, or until the edges just start to turn golden. After 6 minutes, swap the top and bottom sheets to ensure an even bake.
8. Meanwhile, place the chopped hazelnuts on a flat dinner plate and set aside for later.
9. Remove the biscuits from the oven and let them cool for 5 minutes before taking them off the baking paper, then let them cool completely on a cooling rack.
10. Spoon the filling on to the back of 12 biscuits, or pipe it from the edges and then fill the centre. These will be the bases of the sandwiches. Pair each biscuit base with a biscuit top, squeeze them gently together and smooth the filling around the sides of each sandwich with a small spatula or a knife.
11. Holding each sandwich between your thumb and index finger, roll it over the hazelnuts to coat the sides. Place them on the worktop and dust one side with icing sugar, then turn them on to a serving plate and dust the other side. Store in the fridge for up to 2–3 days.

ALSO TRY…

If you prefer your biscuits to retain their crunch for longer, coat their back with a thin layer of chocolate; this will prevent the filling from softening them. In this case, use 80g (2¾oz) chocolate rather than 50g (1¾oz) and do not mix it with the filling: melt it in a microwave instead (two rounds of 30 seconds in an 800W microwave should suffice), then brush it over the back of the biscuits with a pastry brush before piping the filling on.

For an alternative and particularly flavoursome finish, use finely crushed amaretti (see pages 88–90) instead of chopped hazelnuts to coat the sides of the *deliziose*.

Sfogliatelle Frolle

— nut-free

MAKES 12

For the pastry
120g (⅔ cup) caster (superfine) sugar
120g (½ cup) lard or unsalted butter, diced,
    at room temperature
1 tsp vanilla bean paste
zest of 1 organic lemon
⅛ tsp baking ammonia (see page 11)
60g (¼ cup) cold water
300g (3 cups) soft wheat 00 flour, plus
    extra for dusting

For the filling
250g (generous 1 cup) water
⅛ tsp salt
100g (⅔ cup) semolina
180g (¾ cup) ricotta
120g (⅔ cup) caster (superfine) sugar
1 tsp vanilla bean paste
50g (1¾oz) egg (about 1 medium egg)
½ tbsp orange blossom water
1 tsp ground cinnamon
zest of 1 organic orange
30g (¼ cup) candied citron peel, finely
    diced into 5mm (¼in) pieces
30g (¼ cup) candied orange peel, finely
    diced into 5mm (¼in) pieces

For the assembly
1 egg, beaten, for brushing
icing (confectioners') sugar, for dusting

Sfogliatella frolla is a variant of the famous and inimitable *sfogliatella riccia:* the two pastries share the same filling as well as the name, but while in the latter the semolina and ricotta cream is wrapped in a flaky and crunchy shell, in the former it is encased in a soft and crumbly shortcrust pastry. The origins of both pastries date to the 18th century and are deeply rooted in Campania: today, *sfogliatella* is undoubtedly one of the representative sweets of Naples.

    Sfogliatelle are the perfect companions for a Neapolitan espresso, delicious when served at room temperature but unbeatable when eaten warm. They do keep for a day or two, but the pastry will absorb moisture and turn soggy over time, so dig in while they are at their best!

1. The day before baking, place the ricotta in a sieve over a bowl, and keep it in the fridge overnight to drain off any excess liquid.

MAKE THE PASTRY

2. Place the sugar, lard, vanilla, lemon zest and baking ammonia in the bowl of a stand mixer fitted with the paddle attachment. Beat on a medium-high speed for 4–5 minutes until it looks creamy. Add the water and mix for 2–3 minutes, scraping the sides of the bowl a couple of times. The lard mixture will reluctantly incorporate water and might still look curdled. Add the flour and mix to incorporate it fully. Scoop the pastry out of the bowl; it will feel soft and sticky. Wrap it in clingfilm and chill it in the fridge for 1 hour or, better, overnight.

MAKE THE FILLING

3. Weigh the water in a medium pan, add the salt and bring to the boil over a medium heat.

When the water starts to boil, reduce the heat to minimum and add the semolina gradually, sprinkling in a little at a time from above, continuously stirring the water with a whisk to avoid the formation of lumps. When the mixture becomes too stiff for the whisk, mix it with a wooden spoon and keep stirring over a low heat for at least 5–7 minutes to evaporate as much water as possible and produce a dry, thick paste. Take the semolina off the heat, transfer it to a small, shallow tray, line the surface with clingfilm and chill in the fridge until cooled completely.

4. When the semolina has cooled, transfer it to the bowl of the stand mixer fitted with the paddle attachment and beat it on medium speed for a couple of minutes until it looks soft and creamy. Add the ricotta and incorporate it fully at medium speed until smooth and clump-free. Finally, add the sugar, vanilla, egg, orange blossom water, cinnamon, orange zest and candied peels and mix for a few seconds until combined. Scrape the sides of the bowl as needed.

ASSEMBLE

5. Place the pastry on a clean, dry worktop and divide it into 12 equal lumps about 50g (1¾oz) each. Knead each lump of pastry individually: spread it on the worktop with the palm of your hand, then roll it up again and repeat a few times until the texture of the pastry goes from rough and grainy to fine and smooth. Roll the lumps of pastry into 12 balls. Generously flour the worktop, then take a ball of pastry and press it down with the palm of your hand to shape it roughly into a disc, 4–5mm (¼in) thick. Then roll it into an oval, 3mm (⅛in) thick

with a rolling pin. Repeat with all the pieces of pastry.

6. Spoon the filling on the top half of each oval, dividing it evenly across the 12 pieces. Each casing will accommodate about 1 heaped tablespoon of filling. Fold the bottom half of each oval over the filling and seal the edges with your thumbs, squeezing out any trapped air. Using both your hands, gather the filling in the centre of the *sfogliatella*, while pressing down on the pastry edges with the sides of your pinkies to seal them well. Using an 8cm (3¼in) pastry cutter, trim off the excess pastry from the sealed edges, leaving as little border as possible. Brush any excess flour off the *sfogliatelle* with a pastry brush, then transfer them to 2 baking sheets lined with baking paper. Brush the tops with beaten egg, then chill in the fridge for at least 30 minutes. This is not essential, but it helps the *sfogliatelle* retain their shape while baking. (Scan the QR code for a video tutorial.)

7. While the *sfogliatelle* are chilling, place the shelf in the middle of the oven and preheat it to 220°C fan (475°F/Gas mark 9).

8. Give the *sfogliatelle* a second generous coating of beaten egg. Bake the trays separately for 10–11 minutes each until the surface of the *sfogliatelle* are a deep caramel colour. Lightly dust with icing sugar just before serving. Store in the fridge for up to 1–2 days.

Scan here to see how to form, fill and shape *sfogliatelle frolle*.

SMALL & SWEET

Cannoli Siciliani
Sicilian Cannoli

MAKES 12

For the shells
250g (2½ cups) soft wheat 00 flour
1 tbsp unsweetened cocoa powder
20g (generous 1 tbsp) caster (superfine) sugar
1 tsp ground cinnamon
⅛ tsp salt
30g (2 tbsp) lard or unsalted butter, cold
1 large egg, 30g (1oz) for the pastry, the rest
    for brushing
60g (4 tbsp) dry Marsala wine
zest of 1 organic orange
½ tbsp wine vinegar
sunflower or corn oil, for frying

For the cream filling
800g (3½ cups) ricotta, preferably sheep's milk
100g (generous ½ cup) caster (superfine) sugar
1 tsp vanilla bean paste
zest of 1 organic orange
40g (⅓ cup) citron candied peel, finely
    diced (no bigger than 5mm/¼in)
40g (⅓ cup) orange candied peel, finely
    diced (no bigger than 5mm/¼in)

For the assembly
50g (⅓ cup) chopped pistachio kernels
icing (confectioners') sugar, for dusting

Cannoli are undoubtedly the most popular dessert in Sicilian baking. Their name derives from the canes (*canne* in Italian) that were used to mould the shape of the pastry shells. Cannoli are a very old dessert, certainly centuries old, although some historians place their date of birth over one thousand years ago.

Regardless of age, cannoli are a simple yet glorious triumph of flavours. The thin, crispy shell is made with soft wheat flour and lard and flavoured with Marsala wine, orange zest and cinnamon, while the filling is a simple mix of ricotta, sugar and candied citrus peel. The overall amount of sugar is surprisingly small, giving the delicate flavours centre stage.

Traditionally, cannoli are made exclusively with sifted, artisanal sheep's milk ricotta. This is getting harder and harder to get hold of, so if you are not one of the lucky ones that can source it easily, you can use conventional cow's milk ricotta instead. The result may not be as good or in line with the purists' view, but it is still utterly delicious and absolutely worth the calories!

This recipe is not particularly complicated, but a few pieces of equipment are needed: crucially, a pasta maker is essential to roll the dough consistently to the required thickness, and a set of 12 cannoli moulds is indispensable to hold the shape of the shells in the fryer. Cannoli moulds are easily available online or in specialist shops and they consist of open, stainless-steel tubes, typically with a diameter of about 2.5cm (1in).

For the shells to retain their crispy, almost flaky texture, cannoli must be filled at the very last minute. In fact, if you buy them in Sicily, unless you are eating them on the spot, you will be served a set of empty shells and a bowl of filling, so you can fill them at home.

1. The day before making cannoli, place the ricotta in a sieve over a bowl to drain off any excess liquid.

MAKE THE DOUGH

2. Place the flour in a large bowl and sift in the cocoa. Add the sugar, cinnamon and salt and mix with a spoon until fully combined. Dice the lard and add it to the flour mixture. Work the mixture by pinching the pieces of lard with the tips of your fingers to break them into very small lumps, fully coated in flour. Keep working the mixture quickly until the lard is finely dispersed into the flour and no more clumps are visible.

3. Beat the egg in a small bowl and add 30g (1oz) of the beaten egg to the flour mixture. Retain the rest for sealing the shells later. Add the Marsala, orange zest and vinegar and work the mixture in the bowl with your hands. Once all the liquids have been absorbed by the dry mixture, turn it on to the worktop and knead it until all the flour has been incorporated into a smooth dough. The mixture is quite dry, and requires vigorous kneading for a few minutes before all the dry ingredients are incorporated. This will create a rather elastic dough which will need resting before being rolled thin. Wrap the dough in clingfilm and chill it in the fridge for at least 30 minutes, or a couple of hours if possible.

MAKE THE CREAM FILLING

4. Meanwhile, prepare the filling: once drained, shop-bought ricotta can be used as is, artisanal sheep's milk ricotta will need sieving. This can be done by pushing it through the mesh of a strainer with the back of a spoon. Place the ricotta in a large bowl and whisk it with a handheld electric whisk until creamy.

Add the sugar, vanilla and orange zest and whisk to combine. Fold in the candied peels.

5. Transfer the cream to a piping bag fitted with a plain 1.5cm (⅝in) diameter nozzle. Pinch the tip and the back of the bag closed with plastic clips and store it in the fridge until needed.

FRY THE SHELLS AND ASSEMBLE

6. Remove the dough from the fridge, unwrap it and divide it into 4 roughly equal pieces. Flatten one piece with your fingers, then pass it through the rollers of a pasta maker on the widest setting. Fold the pastry in half, turn it 90° and pass it through the pasta maker on the same setting. Repeat the folding and rolling at least 3 more times. Throughout this process the appearance and texture of the dough will change significantly: it will look finer and smoother after each passage. Repeat with the remaining pieces of pastry.

7. Now start laminating the pastry to the required thickness: reduce the gap in the pasta maker rollers by one step and pass the pastry through them once more. Work progressively by reducing the gap and rolling the pastry until it is no more than 1mm (1/32in) thick (usually the thinnest setting on the pasta maker).

8. Using a 12cm (4½in) round pastry cutter, cut 12 discs of dough – 3 from each strip. If such a large pastry cutter is not available, you can also cut the pastry into 12cm (4½in) squares instead. Wrap each disc around a cannoli mould, sealing the overlapping edges with a dab of beaten egg, leftover from the dough. Pinch the dough firmly against the moulds with your thumbs to seal the shells closed. If you cut squares, wrap them around the moulds so

that opposite corners overlap. Do not wrap the dough around the moulds too tightly but leave enough room for it to swell while frying. If the dough is too tightly wrapped around the moulds, the shells are more likely to tear open in the fryer.

9. Set the oil temperature in the fryer to 180°C (350°F) or use a pan large enough to fit at least 2 cannoli shells and fill it with at least 8–10cm (3¼–4in) of oil. Place it over a medium heat, controlling the temperature with a cooking thermometer. While the oil heats up, line a cooling rack with 2 layers of kitchen paper and place it next to the fryer.

10. Fry each shell for no more than 1 minute, turning it over frequently with heatproof tongs or holding it into the oil with a slotted spoon for a few seconds to cook it evenly. Rest the shells on the kitchen paper and remove the cannoli moulds as soon as they are cool enough to handle. The fried shells can be stored, wrapped in paper, for up to 5 days.

11. When you are ready to serve the cannoli, place the pistachios on a dessert plate or in a small bowl. Pipe the cream into both ends of the cannoli, making sure that they are completely filled. Dip each end in the pistachios to coat the cream fully. Arrange on the serving plate and lightly dust with icing sugar. Store in the fridge for up to a day.

TIP

You can prepare the dough up to a couple of days in advance and store it in the fridge, wrapped in clingfilm until needed. The dough can also be frozen.

ALSO TRY...

A very popular variation on the basic recipe includes 60g (2¼oz) chopped dark chocolate chips in the filling. I tend not to add chocolate as I feel that it detracts from the delicate citrus flavour, but this is undeniably the preferred choice of kids.

If you are a pistachio fan, you can blend some of the pistachio butter used for the pistachio cream (see pages 207–8) directly into the ricotta filling and decorate the ends with slivers or dice of candied orange peel: the green and orange contrast will look jewel-like. For a pistachio filling use:

800g (3½ cups) ricotta
100g (generous ½ cup) caster (superfine) sugar
1 tsp vanilla bean paste
60g (2¼oz) grated dark chocolate
100g (scant ½ cup) pistachio butter
(pages 207–8)

Savoury Bakes

Part 3

Piadine

— egg-free
— nut-free

MAKES 8

For the piadine
400g (4 cups) soft wheat 00 flour, plus
    extra for dusting
1 tsp salt
1½ tsp baking powder
60g (¼ cup) lard or unsalted butter, diced,
    at room temperature
180g (¾ cup) lukewarm water

For the filling
80g (2¾oz) rocket (arugula)
200g (7oz) crescenza cheese
16 slices of Parma ham

Piadine are a type of flatbread with an unusually long pedigree: documented references to this type of bread date back to the 14th century with some early evidence of *piadina*-type preparations dating to the Roman Empire. Although today they are a common sight across most of central Italy, accompanied by an array of fillings and often served as a street food, the official birthplace of *piadine* remains Romagna, where they are not only ubiquitous, but also revered as a true institution.

Piadine vary significantly across the region; my version works with a variety of fillings and is thin enough to be folded easily while remaining soft and pliable. The recipe could not get any simpler: the list of ingredients is short, the process is quick and requires no proving, just a brief rest to soften the dough. Traditionally, *piadine* are cooked on flat earthenware, stone slabs or cast-iron frying pans, but a non-stick frying pan serves the purpose just as well.

Piadine can be prepared in advance and stored well wrapped up in clingfilm; however, they are at their best if filled and served freshly made, while still warm. They make the perfect centrepiece for an informal dinner: one where a choice of fillings is shared so each guest can build their own.

I am proposing a very basic filling with Parma ham and crescenza; however, the usual combo of cheese, cured meat and vegetable can be articulated in infinite ways. Robiola, Parmesan, mozzarella, scamorza, Brie, Gorgonzola or, ideally, squacquerone are great dairy fillings, while pretty much any cured meat would do, or even sausage. Options for vegetables, other than almost any salad, are grilled peppers, sautéed mushrooms, fresh or sun-dried tomatoes, caramelised onions or even figs. If you do not fear the wrath of purists, you can even indulge in a *piadina* with chocolate and hazelnut spread while nobody is watching!

MAKE THE PIADINE

1. Add the flour, salt, baking powder and lard to the bowl of a stand mixer fitted with the dough hook. Weigh the water in a spouted jug, then start the mixer on medium speed and slowly trickle the water into the bowl. Continue mixing until the dough looks smooth. The mixer should not work for longer than 3–4 minutes from when you start pouring water into the mixing bowl.

2. Drop the dough on to a clean, dry worktop. Roll it into a sausage shape, divide it in half with a knife or a scraper, then divide each part in half two more times until you have 8 pieces, about 80g (2¾oz) each. Shape each piece

SAVOURY BAKES

into a ball, place it on the worktop, then cover them with a clean dish towel and rest for at least 40 minutes.

3. Flour the worktop generously and roll each ball of dough to a thickness of 2mm (1/16in), shaping it into a disc. You will have 8 discs, about 20–22cm (8–8½in) in diameter. Pile them up in a single stack and cover them again with the dish towel. *Piadine* must be kept covered at all times before and after cooking: keeping them covered until they go in the pan will prevent the dough from drying out, and keeping them covered after they have been cooked will preserve the residual moisture in the dough, keeping the *piadina* supple and warm.

4. Heat a cast-iron flat saucepan or a non-stick frying pan, large enough to fit one *piadina*, over a medium heat. Take one *piadina* out of the pile and pierce it several times with the prongs of a fork. Carefully dust off any excess flour, then place it on the hot pan and cook it for about 2 minutes in total, flipping it over a couple of times to ensure even cooking. The *piadina* is cooked when the pale dough develops the characteristic chocolate brown spots. If the spots are dark brown or black, the *piadina* is overcooked.

5. Cook the remaining *piadine*, piling them up in a single stack on a plate and keeping them covered with a clean dish towel until they are ready to be filled. Despite dusting the flour off the *piadine* before cooking them, some will inevitably gather in the pan: wipe it off with kitchen paper (without scorching your fingers!) or it will burn, making the *piadine* taste bitter.

ASSEMBLE

6. Wash and pat the salad dry. Spread a generous dollop of *crescenza* on each *piadina*, coating only half of the disc. Arrange 2 slices of Parma ham and a small handful of salad over the cheese. Fold the *piadina* in half and serve immediately. Store any leftover unfilled *piadine* in an airtight container for up to 2 days.

ALSO TRY...

You can make a vegan version of *piadine* by swapping the lard with the same amount of extra virgin olive oil, while a less traditional but very appetising alternative can be made by adding 50g (1¾oz) pitted and finely chopped Taggiasca olives to the dough.

— vegan
— egg-free
— dairy-free
— nut-free

Pucce alla Pizzaiola

MAKES ABOUT 32

350g (2½ cups) plain (all-purpose)
    flour, plus extra for dusting
150g (1 cup) strong bread flour
2 tsp dry yeast
1 tsp caster (superfine) sugar
330g (generous 1⅓ cups) warm water
1½ tsp salt, plus ⅛ tsp for the filling
1 large white or yellow onion
120g (4½oz) black olives, possibly Kalamata
2 tbsp capers
3 tbsp extra virgin olive oil
150g (5½oz) passata
⅛ tsp ground black pepper

Pucce are a traditional type of bread from Salento, the heel of the boot-shaped Italian peninsula. They can be plain, and filled with cured meats, cheeses or vegetables, but I like to include fillings in the dough. *Pucce* with olives were initially conceived to provide those working the land with a fulfilling and cheap meal when spending the day out of the house. Today, they are a savoury treat and a ubiquitous street food in all corners of Salento.

The recipe below is from my mother-in-law Giuseppina, who kindly bakes them for me every time I step foot in her home, and it includes the addition of capers and tomatoes as well as the unmissable olives.

The result is a very rustic bread with a bit of a bite, rather than a soft bun. This bread can be consumed on its own as well as eaten to accompany your favourite soup.

1. Add both flours, the yeast and sugar to the bowl of a stand mixer fitted with the dough hook attachment and mix with a spoon until well combined. Start the mixer on medium speed and slowly add the warm water. As soon as the dough comes together in a ball, sprinkle in the 1½ teaspoons of salt and let the mixer incorporate it into the dough. Keep kneading on a medium speed for about 10 minutes until the dough looks smooth and wraps around the hook. Leave the dough to prove in the mixing bowl, covered with clingfilm, until it has doubled in volume; it should take 1 hour at 20°C (68°F).

2. Meanwhile, prepare the filling ingredients: peel and finely dice the onion, slice the olives, rinse the capers under running water and squeeze out any excess water.

3. Heat the oil in a non-stick frying pan over a low heat and shallow-fry the onion for about 5 minutes or until translucent. Stir the onion continuously to avoid browning.

4. When the onion is translucent, add the passata, the ⅛ teaspoon of salt, the pepper and capers and simmer for about 5 minutes, stirring constantly. Simmering the filling will evaporate most of the water. Avoid adding any extra water – the filling should look like a thick paste – to avoid adding too much liquid to the dough in the next step. Remove from the heat and add the chopped olives. Let the filling cool completely, uncovered.

5. Add the filling to the the proved dough and mix it in by folding the dough over it several times until fully incorporated. Leave the dough to prove again for 1½ hours.

6. Meanwhile, line 2 baking sheets with baking paper and dust the worktop with flour.

7. Turn the dough out on to the dusted surface. It will be rather wet, very soft and quite sticky: keep the surface, your hands and a metal scraper coated with a generous layer of flour to facilitate handling. To make 32 evenly sized *pucce*, divide the dough in half, then each half in two quarters, then each quarter into two eighths. Divide each eighth in half twice more: this guarantees an even bake across the batch.

8. Give each lump of dough a round shape by spinning it over a well-floured surface with your fingertips. *Pucce* are not expected to be perfectly shaped, so anything lumpy or slightly misshapen will do! Arrange 16 *pucce* on each baking sheet, spaced evenly apart, and leave them to prove for 30 minutes, uncovered.

9. Preheat the oven to 200°C fan (425°F/gas mark 7).

10. Bake the trays together for 25 minutes. Store the *pucce*, wrapped in paper, for up to 2 days.

ALSO TRY...

My mother-in-law always adds 1 small cored and grated courgette to the filling, and occasionally even 1 diced pepper. I must admit that her richer filling makes *pucce* even tastier. If you do add the additional vegetables, simmer the filling for at least 10 minutes to evaporate as much water as possible.

SAVOURY BAKES

Danubio Salato

SERVES 24
FOR A 30CM (12IN) TIN

500g (3⅓ cups) strong bread flour
3 tsp dry yeast
2 tbsp caster (superfine) sugar
50g (1¾oz) grated Parmesan
1 large egg
270g (scant 1¼ cups) whole milk, warm,
    plus 1 tbsp for brushing
4 tbsp extra virgin olive oil, plus extra
    for greasing
1 tsp salt
150g (5½oz) scamorza affumicata
150g (5½oz) ham
1 egg yolk, beaten, for brushing
50g (generous ⅓ cup) sesame or poppy seeds,
    to decorate

Despite being named after the famous central European river, *danubio* is a quintessentially Neapolitan dish, made with filled brioche bread and shaped as a tear-and-share bake, perfect to be enjoyed during a picnic or kids' birthday parties. It's great to prepare in advance as it may be served both hot and cold.

There are two versions of *danubio*: sweet (*dolce*) and savoury (*salato*): I am going for the latter option, filling the cloud-like bread with a classic ham and smoked scamorza cheese. However, you can let your imagination run wild and fill the rich dough with whatever you fancy: chorizo, smoked ham, pesto, Gorgonzola, anchovies, olive tapenade or creamed dried tomatoes are just a few of the options. For an added element of surprise, mix different fillings in the same tray!

1. Add the flour, yeast, sugar and Parmesan to the bowl of a stand mixer fitted with the hook attachment. Mix with a spoon until fully combined. In a spouted jug, beat the egg with a fork, then add the milk, oil and salt and mix until the salt is fully dissolved. Start the mixer on a low-medium speed and slowly pour in the liquid. Let the mixer knead the dough for about 5 minutes until it is smooth and wraps around the hook.

2. Shape the dough into a ball, then drop it back into the mixing bowl. Cover the bowl with clingfilm and leave the dough to prove until it has doubled in volume. It will take about 3 hours at 20°C (68°F). If your kitchen is very cold, keep the bowl in the closed oven, with the heat off and possibly the internal light switched on.

3. Meanwhile, prepare the filling: dice the cheese into 5–10mm (¼–½in) cubes and cut the ham into small strips. Set aside.

4. Oil the tin: a tart tin, a cake tin or a springform tin all work equally well. Line the bottom with a disc of baking paper. This will help release the *danubio* after baking, particularly if some of the cheese leaks out of the buns.

5. Drop the proved dough on to the worktop and divide it into 24 equal pieces. To ensure that the pieces are roughly the same size, cut the dough in half with a knife or a scraper. Then halve the dough twice more until you have 8 equal chunks of dough. Roll each chunk into a cylinder and divide each cylinder into 3 even-sized pieces.

6. Take a piece of dough, pinch it between your fingers and flatten it to form a round patty, about 8cm (3¼in) diameter. Add a few cubes of cheese and a few strips of ham and pinch the edges while shaping the filled dough to

SAVOURY BAKES

form a small dumpling. Ensure that the edges are well sealed, or the cheese will leak out of the bun when melted. Place the filled dough, sealed side down, into the prepared tin, aligning it to the outer edges. Continue until you have used all the dough and filling. Once the outer rim is complete, fill the inner space with the other dumplings. They should fit snugly in the tin; any space between them will be filled by the dough once proved. Cover with clingfilm and leave to prove for 1 hour.

7. Ten minutes before the proving time is over, move the shelf to the lower half of the oven and preheat it to 180°C (350°F/Gas mark 4).

8. Meanwhile, beat the egg yolk with the tablespoon of milk and delicately brush the surface of the *danubio*. Generously sprinkle the top with sesame or poppy seeds. Bake the *danubio* for 30–35 minutes, or until the top is a deep golden colour.

9. Let the *danubio* cool in the tin for 5 minutes before turning it over a plate, removing the tin and peeling off the baking paper. Store, wrapped in paper, for up to 2 days.

ALSO TRY...

If you are not a fan of cheesy bread, you can omit the grated Parmesan from the flour mix; the recipe will work just as well.

Rotoli di Pizza ai Peperoni
Pizza Rolls with Sweet Peppers

— egg-free
— nut-free

SERVES 20
FOR A 23 X 33CM (9 X 13IN) BAKING TIN

For the dough
450g (3¼ cups) strong bread flour
3 tsp dry yeast
2 tsp caster (superfine) or granulated sugar
250g (generous 1 cup) lukewarm water
3 tbsp extra virgin olive oil
2 tsp salt

For the filling
350g (12oz) red sweet (bell) peppers
   (about 3 medium peppers)
100g (3½oz) red onion (about 1 small onion)
2 tbsp extra virgin olive oil, plus extra
   for greasing
⅛ tsp salt
2 tbsp concentrated tomato purée (paste)
100g (3½oz) green olives, pitted and sliced
ground black pepper, for seasoning
50g (⅔ cup) grated Parmesan
a few fresh basil leaves, roughly chopped

Pizza rolls are a very popular street food and this tear-and-share traybake makes a great and always welcome addition to an informal dinner buffet, a picnic or a kids' birthday party.

Common fillings include the usual tomato sauce, mozzarella and often ham; however, this recipe uses one of my favourite combinations based on ripe red sweet peppers and onions. The vegetables are simmered before being blended to a cream: the cooking brings out their sweetness and makes them easier to digest. The creamed filling also makes a delicious dipping sauce, so don't throw away any leftovers!

MAKE THE DOUGH

1. Add the flour, yeast and sugar to the bowl of a stand mixer fitted with the dough hook and mix them with a spoon until fully combined. Start the mixer on a medium-high speed and slowly trickle the water into the mixing bowl. Immediately after the water, add the oil and continue mixing until the dough comes together evenly. It should take a couple of minutes. Sprinkle in the salt and let the mixer knead the dough for a further 8–10 minutes, or until it becomes smooth, wraps around the hook and comes off the sides of the mixing bowl cleanly.

2. Scoop the dough out of the bowl and, while holding it in your hands, stretch it and fold it over itself a few times and shape it into a ball. Drop it back into the mixing bowl, cut a deep cross on the surface with a sharp knife, cover the bowl with clingfilm and leave the dough to prove until it has doubled in volume; it should take about 1 hour 10 minutes at 20°C (68°F). A very practical solution to prove the dough is to leave the bowl in the closed oven, with the heating off but the internal light switched on. This will generate an optimal draught-free and slightly warm environment to facilitate the action of the yeast. Proving the dough in these conditions may shorten the proving time.

MAKE THE FILLING

3. Meanwhile, prepare the filling: wash the peppers, remove the stems, cores, white pith and seeds, and roughly chop the skin into 2–3cm (¾–1¼in) pieces. There is no need to be accurate as they will be blended

once cooked. Peel and chop the onion, then place it in a medium frying pan with the oil and the chopped peppers. Add the salt and shallow-fry over a medium heat, uncovered, for about 5 minutes, stirring often until the onion has become translucent. Add the tomato purée and about 125g (½ cup) water, cover the pan with a lid, reduce the heat and simmer for about 15 minutes until most of the liquid has evaporated. Keep checking that the pan does not dry out to avoid burning the sauce.

4. Remove the pan from the heat and cream the contents in a heatproof blender or with a stick blender. Set aside to cool.

ASSEMBLE

5. Grease the baking tin, spreading a thin layer of olive oil over the bottom and sides. Line the bottom with a sheet of baking paper.

6. Drop the proved dough over a well-floured surface, roughly shape it into a square with your fingers, then roll it out to a thickness of 5mm (¼in), shaping it into a 30 x 50cm (12 x 20in) rectangle. With the longest side facing you, pour the pepper filling over the dough, and spread it with the back of a spoon or a small offset spatula, leaving 2–3cm (¾–1¼in) of dough at the top of the rectangle sauce-free. Distribute the sliced olives evenly over the dough. Grind a generous dusting of black pepper over the sauce, sprinkle over the grated Parmesan and add the basil leaves. Roll the sheet of dough, starting from the side facing you, all the way to the top.

7. Using a sharp knife, slice the sausage of filled dough into 20 equal rolls, about 2.5cm (1in) thick, and arrange them sideways in the prepared baking tray. There might be space left between the rolls at this stage; however, this will be filled by the dough during the second prove and baking. Leave the rolls to prove again, uncovered, for a further 30 minutes.

8. Meanwhile, set the shelf in the lowest position in the oven and preheat it to 200°C (400°F/ Gas mark 6). Once the second prove is completed, bake the rolls for 27–29 minutes, or until the tops just start to brown. Store, wrapped in paper, for up to a day.

ALSO TRY...

Once you have become familiar with the method, pizza rolls will become one of those basic recipes that you can play with when it comes to fillings: anchovies or Genovese pesto go very well with a basic tomato sauce, but you can also consider unusual tomato-free fillings based on caramelised onions or ricotta and spinach.

SAVOURY BAKES

- vegan
- egg-free
- dairy-free
- nut-free

Focaccia Genovese

MAKES 2 FOCACCE, MEASURING
25 X 40CM (10 X 16IN)

For the dough
360g (generous 1½ cups) lukewarm water
½ tbsp malt extract, clear honey or caster
    (superfine) sugar
300g (3 cups) soft wheat 00 flour (9–12%
    protein content), plus extra for dusting
300g (generous 2 cups) strong bread flour
    (14–15% protein content)
4 tsp dry yeast
2 tbsp extra virgin olive oil, plus extra for
    greasing and brushing
2 tsp salt, plus 2 tsp for sprinkling

For the emulsion
60g (¼ cup) extra virgin olive oil
100g (scant ½ cup) water

When most people think of focaccia, what they are really thinking of is *focaccia genovese*, or *fügassa*. This unassuming bread, flavoured with generous lashings of extra virgin olive oil and salt, is thinner than other types of focaccia and it has a unique texture where crunchy meets soft in the most harmonious way.

This timeless bread is inextricably connected with Genovese culture: once just a cheap and satisfying breakfast for the local fishermen, today it accompanies the most sophisticated meals, dominates the local street-food landscape, and is even dunked in cappuccino for breakfast! A practice which I strongly advise you to try: the contrast between the saltiness of the focaccia and the sweetness of your cappuccino is unmissable.

You can experiment with toppings, but the most common in Genoa is onions: see how to make a *focaccia con cipolle* in the 'Also try...' section. The characteristic dimples on focaccia are not just a decoration: they form little vessels where the oil and the little dusting of flour create a creamy and savoury emulsion, the squashed dough will become very crunchy, and it will contrast with the pillowy crumb surrounding it.

1. This recipe makes almost 1kg (2lb 4oz) of focaccia dough. If your mixer is not large or powerful enough to handle such an amount, either reduce the ingredients proportionally (for example halving the amounts to make only one focaccia), or knead the dough by hand.
2. Measure the water in a spouted jug and dissolve the malt extract in it. Malt extract is very thick, and it takes a while to dissolve in water: drop the spoon with the extract into the water and let it soak for a few minutes before stirring it. Dissolving it will still require vigorous stirring, but the process will be much shorter.
3. Add both flours and the yeast to the bowl of a stand mixer fitted with the dough hook and mix them with a spoon until fully combined. Start the mixer on a low-medium speed, then slowly trickle the malt extract liquid into the mixing bowl. Take your time to do this slowly: it should take almost a full minute. Add the 2 tablespoons of oil immediately after the malt extract water. When the dough comes together into a coarse but coherent mass, sprinkle 2 teaspoons of salt into the mixer bowl and knead the dough on medium speed for 10–15 minutes until it looks very smooth

and it comes off the bowl and hook cleanly, leaving no bits behind. Drop the dough on to a lightly floured worktop. Cover it with the mixer bowl and leave it to rest for 15 minutes.

4. Meanwhile, oil two 25 x 40cm (10 x 16in) Swiss roll tins with 1 tablespoon of extra virgin olive oil each, making sure that the bottoms and sides are fully coated.

5. Divide the rested dough in half with a knife or scraper. Flatten each half with your fingertips, shaping it into a rectangle, about 30 x 15cm (12 x 6in), with the shorter side closest to you. Fold the top third of each rectangle over the centre, then the bottom third over the centre. Put the 2 folded pieces of dough into the tins and press them with your fingertips to stretch the dough as far as it goes; it will not fill the entire tin yet. Cover the tins with a clean dish towel and leave the dough to prove away from cold draughts and direct sunlight until it has doubled in volume. It will take about 50 minutes at 20°C (68°F).

6. Once the dough has proved, spread it further by pressing it down with your fingertips: this time you should be able to cover the entire surface of the tins. Smooth the tops with the palm of your hands and sprinkle 1 teaspoon of salt evenly over each focaccia. Cover them with the dish towel and leave them to prove for a second time for about 40 minutes.

7. While both *focacce* prove, prepare the emulsion: add the oil and water to a glass jar, screw on the lid and shake it vigorously until the oil is fully dissolved.

8. Dust the proved *focacce* lightly with flour, then form the characteristic dimples with your fingers. Rather than using only your fingertips, use half the length of your fingers to form the dimples: press the dough firmly down to squeeze any air out of it. The whole surface should be covered in dimples, but these should be at least a couple of centimetres apart from each other to alternate soft spots with crunchy ones. Pour half the emulsion over each *focaccia* and spread it around with your hands. (If you are making *focaccia con cipolle*, this is the time to scatter the onions.) Leave the *focacce* to prove for a third and final time, uncovered, for about 50 minutes.

9. Set the shelf in the lower half of the oven and preheat it to 240°C (475°F/Gas mark 9).

10. Bake the *focacce* individually for 15 minutes until the top is a light golden colour. As soon as the *focacce* come out of the oven, slide them over a cooling rack and brush over some extra virgin olive oil with a pastry brush to give them extra shine. Store any leftovers, wrapped in paper, for up to a day.

ALSO TRY…

To make 2 *focacce con cipolle*, slice 2 large onions (or 4 small) into 3–4mm (1/8in) slices. Avoid going too thin, or the onion will shrivel to almost nothing in the oven. Mix the onions in a microwave-safe bowl with 1 tablespoon of extra virgin olive oil and a pinch of ground black pepper. Microwave for 1–2 minutes and let cool. When warm enough to handle, scatter over the *focacce* immediately after spreading the emulsion, before the last prove. Bake as above.

SAVOURY BAKES

Crescia al Formaggio
Cheese Loaf

— nut-free

SERVES UP TO 16
FOR A 23CM (9IN) SPRINGFORM CAKE TIN

For the preferment
100g (scant ½ cup) lukewarm water
2 tsp clear honey
2 tsp dry yeast
100g (¾ cup) strong bread flour

For the dough
70g (2½oz) Parmesan
70g (2½oz) Pecorino
300g (generous 2 cups) strong bread flour
4 medium eggs
70g (scant ⅓ cup) extra virgin olive oil
1 tsp ground black pepper
½ tsp grated nutmeg
1 tsp salt

Crescia al formaggio is a savoury, cheesy bread with a soft and lofty crumb, typically baked to celebrate Easter in central Italy. The name relates to *crescere*, i.e. 'grow' in Italian, and it reflects the fact that this bread grows in volume significantly while proving and baking.

There is evidence of this bread documented as far back as the early 19th century in Marche; however, it is a very common bake in Umbria too. It is intended to be served with eggs as a breakfast on Easter morning, or as a starter for a substantial Easter lunch, always accompanied by cured meats and cheeses. Nevertheless, its robust flavour makes it equally good to spice up an unassuming weekday lunch or as a complement for any ordinary soup. Its rich and peppery flavour will be a good excuse for a glass of full-bodied red wine to wash it down.

The characteristic tall and dome-shaped top makes it resemble a panettone, but no special tins are needed as *crescia* can be baked in any conventional springform tin as long as its sides are lined with at least 10cm (4in) wide strips of baking paper.

Some versions of *crescia* call exclusively for mature Pecorino cheese, resulting in a strongly flavoured dough, but I have opted for a slightly more delicate 50/50 split with Parmesan. The airy structure of *crescia* means that it dries out quickly if left unwrapped, so it must be stored in an airtight container.

MAKE THE PREFERMENT

1. Pour the water into a medium bowl, add the honey and mix well with a silicone spatula until the honey is completely dissolved. Choose a bowl much larger than the volume of the preferment as this will grow 3 times while proving. Add the yeast and stir until fully dissolved too. Add the flour and combine with a silicone spatula to make a smooth paste. Clean the sides of the bowl well with the spatula and gather the paste at the bottom of the bowl: any left over on the sides of the bowl is likely to dry out and form flecks of hard dough that will be difficult to dissolve later.

2. Cover the bowl with clingfilm and leave to prove at room temperature, away from cold draughts and direct sunlight. The oven is the ideal place. The preferment should more than triple its volume; this should take about 1 hour at 20°C (68°F). It is ready when its structure is very fluffy and airy, almost foamy, with small bubbles visible on its surface.

SAVOURY BAKES

MAKE THE DOUGH

3. Meanwhile, grate the Parmesan and Pecorino. Given the relatively large amount of cheese, this is best done by blitzing chunks of cheese at high speed in a food processor rather than with a cheese grater.

4. Place the flour in the bowl of a stand mixer fitted with the dough hook. Add the grated cheeses, eggs, oil, pepper, nutmeg and the proved preferment. Start mixing on medium speed. When the dough comes together in a coherent mass, sprinkle in the salt and continue to mix on medium–high speed for about 15 minutes, or until the dough wraps around the hook and comes cleanly off the sides of the bowl.

5. Meanwhile, grease the tin and line the bottom with a disc of baking paper. Cut a sheet of baking paper 20cm (8in) wide and long enough to wrap around the entire tin. Fold the sheet of baking paper in half to make a double-layer 10cm (4in) strip. Line the sides of the tin with this strip, stapling the overlapping ends together to make sure it stays in place.

6. When the dough is ready, scoop it out of the bowl and, while holding it in your hands, gently stretch it and fold it over itself a few times. Shape it into a ball and place it in the prepared tin. Set the shelf in the lowest position in the oven and leave the dough to prove in the oven, with the heat off and the internal light switched on, until the top of the dome is level with the rim of the paper sides. This will take about 2½ hours.

7. Take the proved dough out of the oven, place an ovenproof tray on the bottom of the oven and fill it with boiling water. Preheat the oven to 200°C (400°F/Gas mark 6).

8. Place the baking tin on the shelf, close the oven and immediately reduce the temperature setting to 170°C (340°F/Gas mark 3). Bake for 45 minutes or until the top has a golden, honey colour. A skewer inserted into the middle of the loaf should come out clean. Leave the loaf to cool completely in the tin and only when it is at room temperature, open the sides, peel off the baking paper and move it on to a serving plate. Store, wrapped in paper, for up to a day.

ALSO TRY…

To remain closer to the ancient recipe, swap the extra virgin olive oil for an equal amount of lard, and for an even richer bread, add up to 100g (3½oz) fresh and diced Pecorino to the dough before proving.

Pane Valdostano
Valdostan Loaf

MAKES 2 LOAVES, ABOUT 500G
(1LB 2OZ) EACH

250g (1¾ cups) strong wholemeal flour
250g (scant 2 cups) plain (all-purpose) flour,
    plus extra for dusting and coating
2 tsp dry yeast
320g (generous 1⅓ cups) lukewarm water
15g (1 tbsp) clear honey
20g (generous 1 tbsp) unsalted butter,
    at room temperature
1 tsp salt
150g (1¼ cups) dried figs
80g (½ cup) sultanas (golden raisins)
100g (¾ cup) walnut kernels

As the name suggests, *pane valdostano* is a common sight in bakeries of the Aosta Valley: it is a very rustic, rich and dense loaf, filled with walnuts, dried figs and sultanas. The dough is often made with rye flour, although I prefer the softer and lighter crumb produced by wholemeal flour.

Despite the delicately sweet flavour, which makes it perfect for jams and sugary toppings, this bread also goes surprisingly well with cheeses and cured meats. It is the perfect addition to the breakfast table, and I find it unbeatable simply toasted and covered with a generous helping of salted butter. For the most satisfying experience, however, you must cut yourself a substantial, chunky slice: this loaf is all about the filling and you want to make sure you are getting plenty!

1. Add both flours and the yeast to the bowl of a stand mixer fitted with the dough hook and mix them with a spoon until fully combined. Weigh the water in a spouted jug and dissolve the honey in it. Start the mixer on a medium-high speed and slowly trickle the water into the mixing bowl. Once the liquid has been fully absorbed and the dough has formed a coherent mass, add the butter and continue to mix until this has been fully incorporated. Sprinkle in the salt and mix for about 15 minutes or until the dough wraps around the hook and it comes cleanly off the sides of the bowl.

2. Take the bowl off the mixer, cover it with clingfilm and leave it to prove away from cold draughts and direct sunlight until doubled in volume. This should take about 1 hour at 20°C (68°F). Proving the dough in the oven, with the heat off and the internal light switched on, may shorten the proving time.

3. Meanwhile, prepare the filling. Remove the hard stalks from the figs and roughly chop them into 1–2cm (½–¾in) chunks. Place them, together with the sultanas, in a medium bowl and cover with boiling water. Leave them to soak for 15 minutes, then drain, pat them dry and lightly coat them with 1 tablespoon of plain flour. Chop the walnuts into pieces roughly the same size as the figs.

4. Line a baking tray with baking paper and set aside. Turn the proved dough on to a floured worktop and spread it with your fingers to shape it roughly into a 35cm (14in) square. Scatter the sultanas, figs and walnuts over the dough, distributing the filling evenly.

5. Starting from the side closest to you, roll the dough all the way up to the opposite side. Cut the sausage of filled dough in half, then take one half, flatten it down with the palms of your hands and roll it up tightly along its length to shape it into a slender loaf. Repeat with the other half. Given the large amount of filling, the dough might tear in places when rolling. This is not a problem, and, in fact, it will add to the rustic look of the loaf. Arrange both loaves on the baking tray, keeping them at least 10cm (4in) apart, cover them with a clean dish towel and leave them to prove for a further 45 minutes.

6. Meanwhile, slide a small ovenproof tray on to the bottom of the oven and fill it with boiling water. The steam generated by the water will create a humid atmosphere that will facilitate the rise of the dough while baking. Then set the oven shelf in the lowest position and preheat it to 200°C (400°F/Gas mark 6).

7. When you are ready to bake, cut a single, 2cm (¾in) deep slit lengthways on the top of each loaf, using a razor blade or a very sharp knife. Immediately bake the loaves in the oven for 20 minutes, then reduce the temperature to 180°C (350°F/Gas mark 4) and bake for a further 30–35 minutes or until the crust is a deep caramel colour. Store, wrapped in paper, for up to a day.

ALSO TRY...

If you are after an eye-catching centrepiece for your table, rather than shaping the dough into 2 smaller loaves, bake it as a single piece: the dough will make a gargantuan loaf, about 40cm (16in) long.

Same-day Pizza Margherita

MAKES 4 PIZZAS, 30CM (12IN) DIAMETER

For the dough
200g (scant 1½ cups) strong bread
    flour (14–15% protein content)
500g (3¾ cups) plain (all-purpose) flour
    (10–11% protein content)
2 tsp dry yeast
430g (scant 2 cups) lukewarm water
½ tbsp malt extract or clear honey
3 tsp salt
semolina, for coating the dough, spreading
    and dusting

For the topping
4 mozzarella balls, 125g (4½oz) each
400g (14oz) passata
2 tbsp extra virgin olive oil, plus extra
    for greasing the baking tray
⅛ tsp salt
1 tsp dried oregano (optional)
fresh basil leaves

Pizza margherita is the epitome of Italian culinary and cultural heritage. One of the simplest pizzas, it is still the most popular choice for pizza lovers. My dad always tests pizzerias based on their margherita: he is a firm believer that overcomplicated toppings are merely a way to hide mistakes and that if you want to assess the real value of a *pizzaiolo*, you need to go straight to the basics.

Legend has it that pizza margherita was named after Margherita di Savoia, queen of Italy, in whose honour it was invented, and that the toppings were chosen to match the colours of the Italian flag. Although others have

found evidence of equivalent recipes already mentioned much earlier in the 19th century... Regardless of its origins, its simplicity, versatility and undeniable deliciousness have made it a global success, as well as a favourite of mine.

The list of ingredients is, as is often the case, short and simple: the toppings include good-quality passata, fresh basil, extra virgin olive oil and fresh mozzarella. In theory, only *fior di latte* should be used, which is a type of mozzarella with a lower water content than the version eaten uncooked. However, conventional mozzarella balls sold in brine are perfectly suitable as long as they are left in a colander to drain for 20–30 minutes before use.

The unbeatable flavour and texture of traditional Neapolitan pizza comes from long proving and carefully monitored maturing slots, however, the recipe I use at home when I have to hastily arrange a pizza night, can be whipped up in less than 3 hours start-to-finish, without preferments or long proving times. While this might not deliver exactly the same pizza that you would get from a wood-fired oven, I can guarantee you that my two-stage baking method will deliver the best possible pizza your domestic oven will ever make.

MAKE THE DOUGH

1. This recipe makes almost 1.2kg (2lb 9oz) of pizza dough. If your mixer is not large or powerful enough to handle such an amount, either reduce the ingredients proportionally (for example halving the amounts to make 2 pizzas, rather than 4), or knead the dough by hand.

SAVOURY BAKES

2. Add both flours and yeast to the bowl of a stand mixer fitted with the dough hook and mix them with a spoon until fully combined. Start the mixer on a low-medium speed, then slowly trickle in the water to give time for the flour to absorb it fully. Pouring the water should take no less than a minute. Add the malt extract immediately after the water. When the dough comes together into a coarse but coherent mass, sprinkle in the salt and let the machine incorporate it. Knead the dough on medium speed for 10–15 minutes until it looks very smooth and it comes off the bowl and hook cleanly, leaving no bits behind. Remove the bowl from the mixer and cover it with clingfilm. Keep the bowl away from cold draughts or direct sunlight and let the dough prove until doubled in volume. It will take about 1 hour 10 minutes at 20°C (68°F).

3. Generously dust the bottom of a tray with tall sides (large enough to accommodate 4 balls of dough) with semolina. I use a lidded roasting tray and it works perfectly. A large enough cake carrier does the job very well.

4. Drop the proved dough on to the worktop and divide it into 4 equal pieces with a knife. Flatten and fold each piece on the worktop a couple of times, then roll it into a ball and place it in the tray. Cover the tray with its lid or with clingfilm and leave it to prove for a further 1 hour–1 hour 10 minutes.

ASSEMBLE AND BAKE

5. Meanwhile, prepare your toppings: place the mozzarella balls in a colander over a plate to drain as much liquid as possible. In another bowl, prepare the sauce by mixing together the passata, extra virgin olive oil, salt and oregano (if using).

6. Place the oven shelf in the topmost position, literally under the grill. Place an empty pizza tray or a Swiss roll tray, upside down, on the bottom of the oven. Preheat the oven to the maximum temperature it can reach. The timings below refer to 250°C fan and 280°C fan (in case your oven goes that high). The oven should be turned on at least 30 minutes before starting to bake to make sure that it has reached a steady, high temperature.

7. Oil a baking tray with a small amount of extra virgin olive oil. Spread it by hand around the tray to oil it well, including the sides. The oil should be enough to coat the entire tray, but it should not pool: if it does, remove any excess oil with kitchen paper.

8. Prepare a bed of semolina on the worktop, about 30cm (12in) across. Carefully scoop up one ball of dough and drop it over the semolina bed. Lift the dough from below, ideally with a scraper, do not pinch it or squash it when transferring it to the worktop as this will deflate it. Keep the remaining balls of dough covered while you are spreading your pizza. If left uncovered for too long, they will dry out and form an unpleasant surface crust.

9. Start spreading the dough by pressing it down gently with your fingertips over the bed of semolina: start from the centre and move towards the edges but avoid flattening the borders. This will ensure that your pizza develops a generous, lofty rim while baking. When the dough is about 15–20cm (6–7in) across, lift it up and stretch it further by resting it over the knuckles of your fists and gently moving them apart. Use your fists to slowly

rotate the dough over your hands. Be gentle with the dough to avoid tearing it: very little pulling is needed at this stage as gravity will do most of the work. This action will also ensure that any excess semolina is dusted off the surface of the dough. (Scan the QR code for a video tutorial.)

10. When you have reached 25–30cm (10–12in) in diameter, gently lay the dough over the baking tray and adjust its shape, if necessary. In principle, pizza dough can also be spread with a rolling pin, but the result would not be nearly as good, mostly because the all-important crusty rim would be lost in the process. I recommend transferring the dough to the baking tray just before baking: do not let the dough rest on an oiled baking tray for long or you may struggle to take it off once baked.

11. Spread one quarter of the sauce over the pizza base with the back of a spoon, leaving a 2cm (¾in) border. Spread the sauce over the dough immediately before baking: if the sauce rests on the raw dough for too long, it will soak it and ruin the structure.

12. The pizza is baked in two stages: for the first, pre-baking stage, rest the baking tray on the bottom of the oven, on top of the upside down tray, and bake it for 5 minutes (at 250°C) or for 4 minutes (at 280°C).

13. Take the tray out of the oven and rest it over a heatproof surface. Roughly break up one ball of mozzarella in chunks over the sauce. Do this as quickly as possible as you do not want the pizza to get too cold. Return the pizza to the oven for the second stage of baking, this time under the grill, and bake for a further 4 minutes (at 250°C) or 3 minutes (at 280°C).

14. Remove your pizza from the oven, add a couple of roughly chopped basil leaves, and let it cool for a minute or two in the tray. Slide it on to a chopping board to slice and serve.

15. Bake the remaining pizzas in the same way, oiling the baking tray between bakes. Store any leftovers, wrapped in paper, for up to a day.

ALSO TRY...

Once you have learned the basics of pizza margherita, have some fun and experiment with different toppings. Add them sparingly, though: this method makes a relatively thin base, not strong enough to support the toppings usually found on American-style or deep-pan pizza. Be particularly careful with toppings that release liquids while baking, as they might soak and ruin the dough. When I use mushrooms, for example, I do not wash them in water, but only wipe them with a moist cloth, as they act like sponges and otherwise release a lot of water from the washing on to the pizza when baked.

Apart from the popular topping combinations, my absolute favourites are margherita with Gorgonzola and cherry tomatoes or burrata and 'nduja. For the former: add the halved cherry tomatoes with the sauce and Gorgonzola chunks with the mozzarella. For the latter, add the 'nduja with the sauce and the burrata only once the pizza is already baked.

TIP

Malt extract adds sugars to feed the yeast and flavour the dough. You can use clear honey instead; it will not be as flavoursome, but it will provide the yeast with the sugars it needs.

Scan here to see how to spread a ball of pizza dough.

2

Focaccia Barese

— vegetarian
— egg-free
— nut-free

SERVES UP TO 16
FOR A 30CM (12IN) ROUND TIN

For the dough
290g (scant 3 cups) soft wheat 00 flour
    (protein content 9–12%)
180g (1¼ cups) strong bread flour (protein
    content 14–15%)
2 tsp dry yeast
4 tsp caster (superfine) sugar
200g (scant 1 cup) cold water
140g (generous ½ cup) whole milk, cold
3 tbsp extra virgin olive oil, plus 1 tbsp
    for greasing
2 tsp salt

For the topping
150g (5½oz) cherry tomatoes
100g (3½oz) olives, pitted
1 garlic clove
½ tsp dried oregano
1 tbsp extra virigin olive oil
pinch of salt
pinch of pepper

For the emulsion
2 tbsp extra virgin olive oil
2 tbsp water
½ tsp salt

Focaccia is one of the breads that I love the most. I could easily scoff an entire tray, if I am in the right mood, and the texture of the dough is simply a pleasure to manipulate, not to mention the smell of the marinating tomatoes and olives.

A true *focaccia barese* is typically rather thick, up to 4–5cm (1½–2in), has a very soft

crumb and requires olives from the Bari area in Puglia; however, any savoury, slightly acidic variety, either black or green, works equally well, as long as they are left whole. Any juicy tomato will suit this recipe, better if the variety is in season. I like to use cherry or baby plum tomatoes, but larger, chopped varieties also work. In fact, *focaccia barese* can be made during the winter months even with canned San Marzano tomatoes (peeled and whole). Interestingly, some recipes for *focaccia barese* require the addition of a boiled and mashed potato to achieve a softer, moister crumb. However, I find that adding milk achieves an unparalleled cloud-like texture without compromising the crispiness of the crust.

To achieve the characteristic airy structure of the crumb, the dough must be highly hydrated, which means that the water-to-flour ratio must be relatively high. This will create a very soft and wet dough that might appear fiddly to handle at first, but with a couple of tricks, even the most inexperienced baker will be able to produce a superlative focaccia.

MAKE THE DOUGH

1. Add both flours, yeast and sugar to the bowl of a stand mixer fitted with the dough hook attachment and mix them with a spoon until fully combined. Mix the water and milk in a spouted jug. Start the mixer on medium-high speed and slowly trickle in the liquid. Once the liquid has been incorporated into the flour, add the oil and knead until the dough becomes homogeneous. Sprinkle in the salt and keep mixing for about 15 minutes, or until the dough wraps around the hook and comes cleanly off the sides of the bowl.

GIUSEPPE'S ITALIAN BAKES

SAVOURY BAKES

2. Meanwhile, prepare the topping. Wash, dry and halve the cherry tomatoes, then place them in a small bowl. Add the drained olives, the garlic crushed with a garlic press, oregano, oil, salt and pepper. Mix well and set aside. Preparing and seasoning the topping early gives it time to marinate and soak up all the flavours from the seasoning.

3. Take the bowl off the mixer, cover it with a plate or saucepan lid and let the dough rest for 10 minutes. This will relax the structure and allow the dough to be stretched in the next step.

4. Focaccia dough needs two rounds of lamination: this reinforces the structure and makes even a soft and wet dough easy to handle. For the first lamination, wet your hands and the worktop, and, with the help of a wet plastic curved scraper, turn out the dough on to the wet surface. Gradually stretch the dough as if you were preparing a very large pizza. You should not stretch the dough by pressing it on the worktop, but only by lifting its edges and pulling them progressively. When the dough will not stretch any further and starts to tear, fold the left third over the central third, then fold the right third over the central third. Repeat the folding in a perpendicular direction, then roll up the folded parcel of dough and leave it on the worktop to rest for 15 minutes, covered with the mixer bowl. (Scan the QR code for a video tutorial.)

5. After 10 minutes, repeat the stretching and folding for a second lamination, then drop the dough back into the bowl, cover and let it prove until it doubles in volume. It will take about 1½ hours at 20°C (68°F). Meanwhile,

grease the baking tin with 1 tablespoon of oil, making sure the edges are well oiled.

6. Drop the proved dough into the oiled tin using the plastic curved scraper. Press the dough into the tin with oiled fingers until it covers the entire tin. Cover with clingfilm and prove for a further 30 minutes.

7. Meanwhile, prepare the emulsion. Add the oil, water and salt to a glass jar, screw on the lid and shake vigorously until the salt is dissolved.

8. Take the clingfilm off the tin and, using only the tips of your oiled fingers, create lots of dimples in the focaccia; this will create those delightful pockets of savoury oil while baking. Press the olives and tomatoes into the dough, making sure that they are fully embedded. Pour any leftover marinade over the focaccia. Pour the emulsion evenly over the entire focaccia, and let it prove, uncovered, for 30 minutes.

9. Meanwhile, set the oven shelf in the lowest position and preheat it to 230°C (450°F/Gas mark 8).

10. Bake the focaccia for 17–18 minutes until the top is a light amber colour. Leave to cool in the tin for 5 minutes, then ensure that the sides and bottom are unstuck with a plastic spatula and move your focaccia to a serving board. Store any leftovers, wrapped in paper, for up to a day.

 Scan here to see how to make a lamination for a *focaccia barese*.

— vegan
— egg-free
— dairy-free
— nut-free

Tarallini

MAKES ABOUT 70

500g (5 cups) soft wheat 00 flour, plus
    extra for dusting
2 tsp salt, plus 1 tbsp for boiling
1 tbsp dried fennel seeds, plus extra
    for sprinkling
120g (½ cup) extra virgin olive oil
220g (scant 1 cup) dry white wine

The shelves of almost every single airport shop in Italy are packed with bags of *tarallini*: this crispy snack has almost become the epitome of Italian informal baking and something that every tourist will happily bring back home. Although they can be found anywhere across the country, they mostly originated from the south and especially Puglia, where they are considered a local staple.

    The high oil content, the wine and the double cooking method give *tarallini* a unique and super-crispy texture. This recipe uses the traditional combination of dried fennel seeds, but I must admit that they are satisfyingly good just simple and plain. I would recommend giving the hot chilli version a go and experimenting with different flavours; some ideas are listed in the 'Also try...' section. They are very easy to make and ideal to bake with the kids: the alcohol from the wine will entirely evaporate when baking, so they can safely enjoy them too.

    One batch will make about 70 *tarallini*: this sounds like a lot, but I can assure you that they will be gone in no time. However, if you would rather halve the quantity, I recommend working the dough by hand as it might be just too little for a stand mixer to knead.

Tarallini can be enjoyed any time of the day, with a glass of wine as an aperitif or as finger food for a party. Just be careful, as when you start nibbling them, it is almost impossible to stop...

1. Add the flour, 2 teaspoons of salt and 1 tablespoon of fennel seeds to the bowl of a stand mixer fitted with the dough hook. Mix with a spoon until fully combined. Weigh the oil in a spouted jug.

2. Start the mixer on a low-medium speed and slowly trickle the oil into the bowl. Continue to mix until the oil has been fully incorporated. Scrape the sides of the bowl with a silicone spatula as needed. The mixture will look dry and crumbly. Weigh the wine in the same spouted jug (no need to wash it). Trickle the wine into the bowl, while mixing, and knead the dough on medium speed for about 10 minutes until it looks soft. It should come off the sides of the bowl cleanly. Scoop the dough out of the bowl: it will feel very soft and oily. Wrap it in clingfilm and rest in the fridge for at least 30 minutes.

3. Transfer the rested dough on to a clean, dry worktop and divide it into small lumps, about 10–13g (¼oz) each. There is no need to be overly accurate: I roll the dough into a long, 2cm (¾in) thick noodle and cut it into evenly sized lumps. If you obtain 70–80 lumps, then you know that the weight is in the right ball park. Lightly flour a large area of the worktop for the shaped dough. Roll each lump of dough between your hands to shape it into an 8–10cm (3¼–4in) long noodle, wrap it loosely around your index finger to form a ring and

GIUSEPPE'S ITALIAN BAKES

pinch the overlapping ends together with your thumb and index finger. Arrange the rings on the floured surface while you work through the remaining dough. This may seem time-consuming at first, and you will probably have to rework a few to get them right, but once you become familiar with the process, it will get faster and more satisfying.

4. Once all the *tarallini* are shaped, pour about 2 litres (70fl oz) of water into a large pan, add 1 tablespoon of salt and bring it to a fast boil. Lay a large, clean dish towel over the worktop next to the pan. Set the shelf in the middle of the oven and preheat it to 190°C (375°F/Gas mark 5). Line a baking sheet with baking paper.

5. Boil the *tarallini* in small batches of 8–10: drop them in the boiling water and scoop them out with a slotted spoon only when they rise to the surface. It takes no more than a couple of minutes to cook one batch. Rest the cooked *tarallini* on the dish towel. Their texture will change significantly upon boiling from very soft to almost rubbery. Resist the temptation of boiling too many at once, as they tend to stick together in the water, and you might end up with one, large lump of dough rather than a set of beautifully cooked *tarallini*.

6. As soon as you have boiled them all, transfer them to the baking sheet, keeping them 1–2cm (½–¾in) apart. You should be able to fit about 30 *tarallini* on a standard baking sheet. Sprinkle extra fennel seeds over the *tarallini* to decorate. Bake each batch for 40–42 minutes or until the surface starts to turn golden. Store in an airtight container for up to a week.

ALSO TRY...

Tarallini can be flavoured with your favourite herbs and spices: for an aromatic snack, swap the fennel seeds for 1 tablespoon of fresh, finely chopped chives or rosemary. For a fiery alternative, use ½ teaspoon of ground black pepper or ⅛ teaspoon of hot chilli powder; in this case, you can add also ½ teaspoon of paprika to the dough for colour and sprinkle extra on the boiled *tarallini* to decorate them.

If you have the chance, leave the boiled *tarallini* uncovered to dry out at room temperature overnight before baking them: the resulting texture will be even crispier!

Rustici Leccesi

MAKES 6

For the béchamel sauce
220g (scant 1 cup) whole milk
20g (generous 1 tbsp) unsalted butter
20g (generous 1 tbsp) plain (all-purpose) flour
⅛ tsp salt
⅛ tsp ground black pepper
⅛ tsp freshly grated nutmeg

For the pastry cases
800g (1lb 12oz) puff pastry (pages 212–13)
plain (all-purpose) flour, for dusting

For the assembly
50g (1¾oz) mozzarella for pizza (see intro)
50g (1¾oz) passata
1 tsp extra virgin olive oil
pinch of salt
1 egg white, beaten

Rustici leccesi are medallions of flaky puff pastry filled with a cheesy sauce and with a hint of tomato. They can be bought in every bakery or bar in Salento, the southernmost region of Puglia, where they originated and represent the epitome of local street food. The size is rather generous, and it has to be in order to accommodate (and properly seal within) enough filling. In principle, one *rustico* is large enough to be worthy of a light meal, although they are so appetising and easy to eat that most people consume them throughout the day as a savoury treat, especially in the summer.

This recipe uses two thirds of the batch of homemade puff pastry (pages 212–13), although a shop-bought equivalent (chilled or frozen)

would be perfectly suitable too. Whether you use homemade or shop-bought, chilled or thawed puff pastry, always leave it at room temperature for 1 hour before unwrapping it to avoid the formation of unwanted condensation on the dough.

If using shop-bought pre-rolled pastry, a batch of *rustici* can literally be whipped up in minutes; the recipe is quite simple and forgiving. The key to success is to avoid excessive moisture in the filling: the dreaded soggy bottom is just around the corner! I suggest using mozzarella for pizza for this recipe, i.e. the type sold as blocks in vacuum-sealed packages, rather than the traditional balls sold in brine, as the former releases less liquid when melting.

One final recommendation: *rustici leccesi* must be eaten hot to savour the creaminess of the filling in its full glory; however, cold *rustici* can be reheated in a hot oven for 6–8 minutes.

MAKE THE BÉCHAMEL SAUCE

1. Bring the milk to a gentle simmer in a small saucepan. Meanwhile, melt the butter in another small saucepan, add the flour in one go, keeping it over a very low heat, and mix with a wooden spoon to make a paste. As soon as the milk starts to simmer, pour it into the butter and flour mix in stages, mixing vigorously. Only add more milk when the previous milk has been fully incorporated. Once you have added all the milk, keep simmering over a very low heat until the sauce looks smooth and creamy, then season it with the salt, pepper and nutmeg. If there are any lumps, they usually dissolve by mixing the

sauce for a little longer. A whisk is a great help here.

2. The sauce can be prepared in advance, so if you are not using it immediately, transfer it to a bowl, line the surface with clingfilm and store it in the fridge until needed.

ASSEMBLE

3. While the béchamel sauce is cooling, prepare the other fillings: grate or dice the mozzarella and season the passata with the oil and salt.

4. Line a baking sheet with baking paper. Avoid using silicone mats as they take longer to heat up, which may result in a pastry with a less flaky or worse, doughy, bottom. Fit the shelf in the lowest position in the oven and preheat it to 200°C (400°F/Gas mark 6). Placing the tray closer to the bottom heating element in the oven ensures that the pastry bases will be fully baked by the time the tops are puffed up, and that any residual moisture coming from the filling is fully dried out.

5. To make the pastry cases, generously flour the worktop and roll the puff pastry into a rectangular sheet, 3mm (⅛in) thick. With a 12cm (4½in) round pastry cutter, cut out 12 discs of pastry. If you do not have such a large pastry cutter available, you can cut the discs with a pizza cutter or a knife, using a suitably sized bowl or saucer as a template.

6. Make the pastry bases by thoroughly coating the top of 6 discs with the egg white. Drop 1 heaped tablespoon of béchamel sauce, a few cubes of mozzarella and 1 teaspoon of passata in the centre of each pastry base. Make sure you leave at least 2cm (¾in) of empty pastry around the border of each base.

7. Place the remaining discs over the filled pastry bases, moulding them carefully so that there are no wrinkles of pastry around the edges. At this stage, slide your fingers around the edges of the pastry, to ensure that the top discs are in full contact with the bottom discs, but do not apply any pressure, as this will stop the edges from puffing up during baking.

8. Gently push the back (i.e. the blunt side) of an 8cm (3¼in) round pastry cutter over the domed centre of each pastry, sealing the filling in place to ensure it does not leak while baking. Give the pastry cases a final brush of egg white and cut a 1cm (½in) wide slit in the centre of each dome to allow the steam to escape without bursting the pastries open.

9. Bake for 30–32 minutes or until the tops are a deep amber colour. Serve while still warm. Store any leftovers, wrapped in paper, for up to a day.

FOR THE PASTRY
— vegan
— egg-free
— dairy-free
— nut-free

Tiella

SERVES UP TO 8
FOR A 27CM (10¾IN) TART TIN

For the dough
400g (3 cups) plain (all-purpose) flour
(10% or less protein content), plus extra
for dusting
1½ tsp dry yeast
1½ tsp caster (superfine) or granulated sugar
180g (¾ cup) lukewarm water
40g (3 tbsp) dry white wine
2 tbsp extra virgin olive oil
1½ tsp salt

For the filling
Prepare one batch of filling using the quantities
and methods on pages 196–201. Fillings can
be prepared in advance and stored in a sealed
container in the fridge until needed.

For the assembly
½ tbsp oil for greasing the tin, plus extra
for brushing

Tiella is the gastronomic masterpiece of Gaeta,
my hometown. I would be disowned by the
entire town (not to mention my parents and
extended family) if I did not include a version
in this book. But I am not doing it only as an act
of respect to my ancestors: I am convinced
that, if you love savoury bakes as much as I do,
this versatile recipe will introduce you to an
entire world of new culinary experimentations.

Similarly to the well-known Cornish pasty,
tiella was designed to fill a need and provide
fishermen and land workers with a portable
lunch when they had to spend their day away

from home. A *tiella* is essentially a stuffed pie,
where a savoury filling is sandwiched between
two thin layers of yeasted pastry. The dough
might look similar to a conventional pizza
dough; however, there are a few small, critical
differences that set it apart and give it a very
peculiar and unmistakable texture.

A traditional *tiella* is a round, large pie,
served in single-serving slices, which can be
enjoyed either hot or cold. It is best baked in
a round tin with fluted sides to help layer the
dough and filling, and to make crimping the
edges easier. A straight-sided tart tin could be
used too, but it will make the job slightly fiddlier.

Apart from the oil, wine and sugar, which are
not usually added to the typical pizza dough,
the main peculiarity of *tiella* dough is that it is
made with a low-protein content flour (i.e. not
a strong, bread or a Canadian-type flour) and it
is kneaded for a relatively short time. This is to
keep the gluten content as low as possible and
deliver a pastry with a crisp, soft and almost
flaky texture.

In fact, the many *nonnas* I have spoken to
have confided that the secret to the perfect
tiella dough is to knead it by hand, as the action
is much gentler than that of a stand mixer. So,
if you enjoy getting your hands covered in flour
and want to give it a bit of elbow grease, now
you have a very good excuse to!

Typical fillings are based on what was
cheap and readily available in pantries back
in the day, so usually vegetables, fish or a
combination thereof. The recipe below gives
you the ingredients and method for making a
generic *tiella*; you can then match it with your
favourite filling out of those proposed next, with
meat (pages 197–9), fish (page 201) and vegan

(page 196) options available. Nowadays, *tiella* is also a great solution for emptying your fridge of whatever ingredients need using up. I truly hope that, once you have learned the basics, you will start exploring different filling combinations to concoct your very own *tiella* recipe.

MAKE THE DOUGH

1. Add the flour, yeast and sugar to the bowl of a stand mixer fitted with the dough hook and mix well with a spoon until fully combined. Mix the lukewarm water and wine in a spouted jug. Start the mixer on a low-medium speed and slowly pour the liquid into the mixing bowl. Adding the liquid slowly and continuously makes the incorporation of the water and wine into the flour quicker. The mixer would have to work for longer to incorporate the liquid if this was added in one go, producing a tougher pastry. Add the oil immediately after the water and wine and let the mixer incorporate it into the dough. As soon as the dough comes together in a ball, sprinkle in the salt and let the mixer incorporate it. Knead the dough until it looks smooth and wraps around the hook. Overall, the mixer should not work for longer than 4–5 minutes from when you start pouring in the water/wine.

2. Scoop the dough out of the bowl and, while holding it in your hands, fold it over itself a few times and shape it into a ball. Drop it back into the mixing bowl, cut a deep cross on the surface with a sharp knife, cover the bowl with clingfilm and leave the dough to prove until it has doubled in volume; it should take about 1 hour 10 minutes at 20°C (68°F).

ASSEMBLE AND BAKE

3. Set the shelf in the lowest part of the oven and preheat it to 180°C (350°F/Gas mark 4). Oil the tart tin with ½ tablespoon of extra virgin olive oil, making sure that the edges are very well oiled too. Set aside.

4. Drop the proved dough on to a floured surface and divide it into 2 pieces, one slightly larger than the other. Roll the larger piece of dough into a 2mm (1/16in) thick disc using a rolling pin. Flour the dough liberally to ensure that it does not stick to the surface or to the rolling pin. I find using 2mm (1/16in) rubber spacer rings on both ends of the rolling pin very helpful, as it stops me from spreading the dough too thin. Wrap the entire disc of dough around the rolling pin and unroll it over the prepared tin. Adjust the dough to ensure that it snugly lines the bottom of the tin. Let the excess dough hang over the edges.

5. Spoon the filling into the tin, spread it evenly over the dough and flatten it down with the back of a fork. Ideally, the filling should be 1–1.5cm (½–5/8in) thick.

6. Roll the remaining dough into a 2mm (1/16in) thick disc and, using the same technique as above, unroll it over the tin. Gently seal the edges of the *tiella* by pressing the dough against the flared sides of the tin with your thumbs. Trim off the excess dough by running a blunt knife along the rim of the tin. Crimp the edges of the *tiella* by pushing the dough down at regular intervals around the tin, creating a scalloped profile. (An alternative, and equally attractive, option is to simply seal the edges of the *tiella* by pressing it against the flared sides of the tin with the prongs of a fork.)

7. Liberally sprinkle a couple of tablespoons of olive oil over the top disc of dough and spread it either by hand or with a pastry brush. Create several holes in the top layer of pastry by pushing a fork through the top disc to create vents for the steam to escape while baking.

8. Once filled and sealed, bake the *tiella* immediately to avoid any liquid from the filling soaking the bottom layer of dough. Bake the *tiella* for 40 minutes–1 hour until the pastry looks golden and the crimped edges just begin to brown. The baking time depends also on the filling: octopus *tiella* takes longer to bake, up to 1 hour; vegetable fillings bake in 40–45 minutes. Before removing the *tiella* from the oven, gently lift one corner with a spatula and make sure that the bottom is fully cooked and golden. Store in the fridge for 2–3 days or freeze for up to a month.

TIP
A very practical solution to prove the dough is to leave the bowl in the closed oven, with the heating off but the internal light switched on. This will generate an optimal draught-free and slightly warm environment to facilitate the action of the yeast.

SAVOURY BAKES

Calzoni

FOR THE PASTRY
— vegan
— egg-free
— dairy-free
— nut-free

MAKES 6

For the dough
270g (2 cups) plain (all-purpose) flour (10% or less protein content), plus extra for dusting
1 tsp dry yeast
1 tsp caster (superfine) or granulated sugar
120g (½ cup) lukewarm water
30g (2 tbsp) dry white wine
1½ tbsp extra virgin olive oil
1 tsp salt

For the filling
Prepare one batch of filling using the quantities and methods on pages 196–201. Fillings can be prepared in advance and stored in a sealed container in the fridge until needed.

For the assembly
extra virgin olive oil, for brushing

If *tiella* (pages 189–92) is ideal for a picnic or a meal outdoors where many people will be sharing food, *calzoni* are perfect, self-contained single servings. They are simply the folded version of *tiella* and they share the same dough ingredients and method.

The quantities in this recipe have been adjusted to make six single-serving *calzoni*, but the method is identical to that for *tiella*. As for *tiella*, you can choose your favourite filling for your *calzoni*. One batch of filling prepared according to the quantities and methods on pages 196–201 will be just enough to fill the six parcels of dough.

MAKE THE DOUGH

1. Prepare the *calzoni* dough following the same method as the *tiella* (pages 189–92).

ASSEMBLE AND BAKE

2. Drop the proved dough on to a floured worktop and divide it into 6 equal pieces, about 70g (2½oz) each. Shape each piece into a small ball and prove for 20 minutes, covered with a clean dish towel.
3. Line a baking sheet with baking paper. Place the shelf in the middle of the oven and preheat it to 180°C (350°F/Gas mark 4).
4. Roll each ball of dough to a thickness of 2mm (¹⁄₁₆in), shaping it into a disc about 20cm (8in) in diameter. Flour the dough and the worktop to make sure that it does not stick.
5. Spoon the filling on to the lower half of each disc, dividing it evenly between the 6 discs. Lightly wet the edges of each disc with a pastry brush dipped in water and fold the top half over the bottom half to create the typical half-moon shape. Seal the borders by pressing the lips of dough together with your fingers.
6. Crimp the round edges of each *calzone* by pushing the dough down at regular intervals. Arrange the *calzoni* on the baking sheet and drizzle with extra virgin olive oil. Spread the oil over the surface with your fingers or a pastry brush and bake for 35–40 minutes, or until the pastry looks golden and the crimped edges just begin to brown. The octopus *calzoni* take slightly longer, so they might need the full 40 minutes baking. Store in the fridge for 2–3 days or freeze for up to a month.

SAVOURY BAKES

Ripieno di Spinaci e Pinoli
Spinach and Pine Nut Filling

— vegan
— egg-free
— dairy-free

MAKES ENOUGH FILLING FOR 1 TIELLA
OR 6 CALZONI

600g (1lb 5oz) fresh spinach
⅛ tsp salt, plus extra to taste
80g (2¾oz) pitted Gaeta or Kalamata olives
1 garlic clove
½ chilli
2 tbsp pine nut kernels
3 tbsp extra virgin olive oil

Like other vegetable-based fillings, this spinach and pine nut option lends itself to be eaten cold and is an excellent choice for a lunch outdoors. I am very partial to pine nuts, and although I have restrained myself to just a couple of tablespoons in this recipe, I must admit that I often add as many as I have available. My grandmother used to add a couple of tablespoons of soaked raisins to the mix too. I am not a fan, so I have omitted them from this recipe; however, the contrast between the sweetness of the raisins and the saltiness of the olives makes an interesting combination, in case you are brave enough to experiment.

1. Wash the spinach in plenty of cold water. Add 2–3cm (¾–1¼in) of water to a large pan, bring to the boil and add the spinach. Add the salt, cover the pan with a lid and simmer for 6–7 minutes, stirring at least a couple of times, until the spinach is fully wilted. Drain the spinach in a colander and leave to cool.
2. Meanwhile, drain and halve the olives, crush the garlic, remove the seeds and white pith from the chilli and chop the skin finely.
3. When the spinach is cool enough to handle, squeeze out the water, one handful at a time, and place in a medium bowl.
4. Using a fork, loosen up and untangle the spinach leaves, then add the olives, garlic, chilli, pine nuts and olive oil. Mix well. The mixture should not need any extra salt but check just in case and add a pinch if needed. Store in the fridge for up to 2 days.

ALSO TRY...
This spinach filling goes extremely well with stockfish or tuna: you can make an easy fish alternative to the basic recipe by adding a 100g (3½oz) can of drained and flaked tuna to the mix. And if you are not a fan of olives, replace them with 100g (3½oz) goat's cheese, broken into large chunks for a very sophisticated flavour.

My great aunt Vera strongly recommends swapping spinach for chard for a sweeter alternative, which can be easily heated up by a more generous amount of hot chilli.

— egg-free
— nut-free

Ripieno di Cipolle
Onion Filling

MAKES ENOUGH FILLING FOR 1 TIELLA OR
6 CALZONI

500g (1lb 2oz) white onions
250g (9oz) cherry or baby plum tomatoes
100g (3½oz) pitted Gaeta or Kalamata olives
½ hot chilli
50g (1¾oz) air-dried salami (*piccante*,
    if preferred)
¼ tsp salt
50g (⅔ cup) grated Parmesan
a few fresh basil leaves, chopped
⅛ tsp ground black pepper
4 tbsp extra virgin olive oil

The onion filling is the 'poorest' option out of those proposed here: certainly the cheapest in terms of cost, it is by no means poor in flavour. In fact, the onion filling typically ranks as one of the highest in the general (informal) polls conducted around our kitchen table.

   A couple of simple precautions must be taken to drain the onions of any potential bitter aftertaste and it certainly helps using white onions, rather than yellow or red.

1. Peel the onions and slice them finely: slices should be 2–3mm (¾–1¼in) thick at most. Place them in a heat-resistant bowl, cover them with freshly boiled water and leave them to soak for 1 hour.
2. Meanwhile, prepare the other ingredients: wash, dry and halve the tomatoes, drain and halve the olives, remove the seeds and white pith from the chilli and chop it finely, and dice the salami into small cubes.
3. Drain the onions and place them in a large frying pan, add the tomatoes and salt, cover the pan with its lid and place it over a medium heat. Simmer for about 5 minutes or until the onions look translucent, then remove the lid and simmer for a further 5 minutes or until all the liquids have evaporated. If there is any leftover liquid in the pan but the onions look fully cooked, take them off the heat and drain the liquids.
4. Let the onions cool completely, and only when they are at room temperature, add the olives, chilli, salami, Parmesan, chopped basil leaves, pepper and oil. Mix well until fully combined. Store in the fridge for up to 2 days.

ALSO TRY...
For a milder taste, you can swap up to half of the onions with leeks or spring onions (scallions).

Ripieno di Broccoletti e Salsiccia
Rapini and Sausage Filling

— egg-free
— dairy-free
— nut-free

MAKES ENOUGH FILLING FOR 1 *TIELLA* OR
6 CALZONI

150g (5½oz) pork shoulder
150g (5½oz) pork belly
⅔ tbsp coriander seeds, bashed
    in a pestle and mortar
⅛ tsp hot chilli powder
½ tsp paprika
½ tsp salt
50g (3½ tbsp) dry white wine
400g (14oz) tenderstem broccoli (broccolini)
4 tbsp extra virgin olive oil
1 garlic clove

Broccoletti or *rape* are a very popular vegetable, grown and loved in central/southern Italy where it has become the basis of some of the most celebrated regional dishes. *Broccoletti* are often paired with spicy pork sausage to make a classic casserole, which also doubles up as irresistible street food, when served in a bun: the combination of *broccoletti* and *salsiccia* is the proverbial marriage made in heaven.

It was only a matter of time, then, before they would find their way into *tiella* or *calzoni*: in fact, as a filling for these stuffed pies, the use of *broccoletti* and *salsiccia* is relatively recent, but it has quickly become many people's favourite. And you will easily understand why the minute you try it for the first time!

Exporting this recipe out of its native regions, however, is no easy task: in principle, for the combination to really work, you need to use the right type of vegetable and the right type of sausage, both rather difficult to find outside Italy. The challenge for me was to come up with a *broccoletti* and *salsiccia* filling without *broccoletti* or *salsiccia*!

So I went on a hunt to find the closest alternatives and I was surprised by how good the end result was when I first tested it. *Broccoletti* are also known as *rape* or *rapini*: they are a leafier relative of broccoli, but with smaller florets and a more delicate taste. If you cannot find them, broccolini or tenderstem broccoli are a perfect alternative and much easier to find.

As far as the meat is concerned, I had to go straight to the root of the problem: if the appropriate sausage is difficult to find, then why not use exactly the same cuts of meat and, crucially, the same blend of spices that would have gone into the casing instead? Adding those 'building blocks' into the main body of the recipe works really well and it has given me the chance to export one of the most loved Italian flavours beyond the Alps.

1. The day before baking, marinate the meats: dice the pork quite finely so that each piece is no larger than 1cm (½in), then add it to a bowl with the coriander seeds, chilli powder, paprika, salt and wine. Mix well until fully combined, then cover with clingfilm and leave in the fridge to marinate until the following day.
2. The following day, wash and drain the tenderstem, then chop them into 5cm (2in) long pieces. Leave the end with the floret and the thinner stems whole but slice the thickest stems in half lengthways to ensure even cooking.
3. Drizzle the oil into a large frying pan and crush the garlic in with a garlic press. Gently fry the garlic over a low heat for a few seconds until

just golden, then add the meat and the juices of the marinade. Sauté the marinated meat over a medium heat for about 7–8 minutes until all the liquids released by the meat have evaporated and the meat starts to fry. This will also toast the coriander seeds, enhancing their flavour.

4. Add the tenderstem, reduce the heat to minimum, cover the pan with its lid and simmer for about 30 minutes. Check the pan often as you will probably need to add a couple of tablespoons of water to keep it simmering.

5. When the vegetables are almost cooked, remove the lid and let the excess water in the filling (if any) evaporate completely. The vegetables are fully cooked when they are soft and you can easily insert a fork into the thickest stem. Make sure that there are no liquids pooling at the bottom of the pan or these will soak the dough and produce the dreaded soggy bottom.

6. As a last step, check the filling for salt: it should not need any more, as the marinade will have seasoned the meats sufficiently, but just in case, this is your last chance to adjust it with an extra pinch. Let the filling cool to room temperature before adding it to the *tiella* or *calzoni*. Store in the fridge for up to 2 days.

TIP

You may decide to leave the coriander seeds whole; however, I strongly recommend giving them a good bash with a pestle and mortar: not only will this avoid the unpleasantness of biting into a large seed, but it will also help release their flavour.

ALSO TRY...

If you are feeling adventurous and do not mind a little extra heat, double up the amount of hot chilli powder and/or add chilli flakes. This filling is at its best when it is fiery.

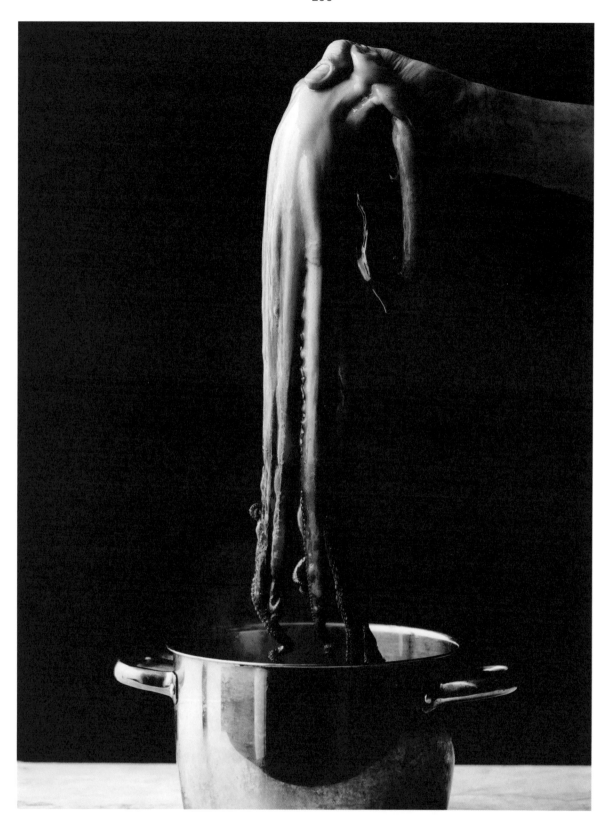

— egg-free
— dairy-free
— nut-free

Ripieno di Polpi
Octopus Filling

MAKES ENOUGH FILLING FOR 1 TIELLA OR 6 CALZONI

800g (1lb 12oz) fresh octopus, cleaned, gutted and washed
150g (5½oz) tomatoes
80g (2¾oz) pitted Gaeta or Kalamata olives, sliced
1 garlic clove, crushed
½ hot chilli, deseeded and finely chopped
bunch of fresh parsley (about 15g/½oz)
3 tbsp extra virgin olive oil
¼ tsp salt

Tiella with octopus is undoubtedly the queen of *tielle*: fish is the expensive filling that originally would be used in a *tiella* either to celebrate a special event or to be given as an exclusive present to a respected friend. This filling, however, lends itself perfectly well to be wrapped in *calzoni* too. As a matter of fact, it is also delicious eaten on its own, cold, as a tasty starter to a celebratory meal.

As with most other fillings, this must be kept as dry as possible to avoid the dreaded soggy bottom: very juicy tomatoes like cherry or baby plum must be avoided, and only the flesh of seeded and cored larger salad tomatoes, such as San Marzano, should be used instead.

This filling is pre-cooked and the octopus requires a long cooling time, so it is best prepared in advance and stored in the fridge until needed. When buying the octopus, consider that one third gets lost by gutting it, so in order to have 800g (1lb 12oz) of cleaned octopus for this recipe, you should buy about 1.3kg (3lb) whole.

1. The day before baking, cook the octopus: bring about 5cm (2in) of water to a fast boil in a wide pan. Slowly lower the octopus into the boiling water, one piece at a time; wait for the water to start boiling again before adding the next piece. The water should be barely enough to cover the octopus, as it will shrink and release more liquid while cooking. Wait for the water to start boiling again, then cover the pan with a lid, reduce the heat and simmer for 30–45 minutes, depending on the thickness of the flesh. Occasionally turn the pieces of octopus to ensure even cooking. The octopus is ready when you can comfortably insert a fork into the thickest section of a tentacle.

2. Remove the pan from the heat but leave the octopus in the water, covered with the lid, until it is has cooled to room temperature, preferably overnight. This step is critical to complete the cooking and ensure that the octopus is tender. Undercooked or hastily cooled octopus will be rubbery and chewy.

3. On the day of baking, wash and dry the tomatoes. Quarter each one and remove and discard the core and seeds. Dice the fleshy skin and drain off any excess water.

4. Lift the cold octopus from the water and dice it rather finely: each piece should be smaller than 1cm (½in). Discard any leftover entrails. Place the octopus in a colander and leave to drain for 20–30 minutes, stirring occasionally to make sure that all excess liquid is drained.

5. Finally, prepare your filling by mixing the octopus, tomatoes, olives, garlic, chilli, parsley, oil and salt until fully combined. Store in the fridge for up to 2 days.

Basics

Part 4

Crema Pasticcera
Pastry Cream

gluten-free
nut-free

MAKES ABOUT 700ML (24FL OZ)

1 organic lemon
500g (2 cups) whole milk
1 tsp vanilla bean paste
75g (2½oz) egg yolk (about 5 medium egg yolks)
110g (scant ⅔ cup) caster (superfine) sugar
50g (½ cup) cornflour (cornstarch)
small pinch of salt

Crema pasticcera or pastry cream is a very versatile basic, good enough to be served as a dessert on its own (perhaps garnished with Amarena cherries or caramelised nuts), but more often called upon by other cakes or pastries as a filler or a coating. In this book, the basic pastry cream is used as a filling for *pasticciotti* (pages 113–115) and *zeppole* (pages 127–31), the coffee version is used in the hot milk and coffee sponge cake (pages 37–9) while the orange version fills the layers of the celebration cake (pages 72–8). Nevertheless, mastering the making of a good *crema* will unlock many other recipes and give you the opportunity to play with flavour and texture to create your own unique bakes.

The method is simple; the only potential problem is unwanted curdling of the cream, but if you follow the steps carefully, you are guaranteed excellent results with little effort. I am so convinced of the success rate of this recipe that I have eliminated sieving the cream once ready (which most bakers do), as I am sure that you will be left with no unwanted lumps.

The basic version of the cream is only lightly vanilla flavoured; a hint of lemon is added mostly to balance out the eggyness and it is hardly noticeable, making it a suitable match for pretty much any other flavour. The basic version can be flavoured in many ways: I have included orange, chocolate and coffee options.

The stiffness of the cream is controlled by the amount of cornflour added, and I have fine-tuned this in the different versions to give you a very smooth, silky texture. Bear in mind that the cream will appear rather thin when still hot, but will thicken significantly upon cooling. However, if you want to make it thicker, slightly increase the amount of cornflour, but go easy: cornflour is a very powerful thickener and overusing it may produce a stodgy, rather than silky, cream.

The ingredients above will make more than enough cream to fill one *torta della nonna* (pages 23–5), one batch of *pasticciotti* (pages 113–15), or one layer of filling in a 23–25cm (9–10in) round cake. To fill the celebration cake (pages 72–8), which requires two layers of cream, use about 1½ times the quantities above, while to fill a set of 12 *zeppole* (pages 127–31), double the amounts.

1. If you are using the lemon, peel it, making sure to shave only the yellow skin, leaving the white pith on the fruit.
2. Place the milk, vanilla and lemon peel in a pan and gently bring to a light simmer. Meanwhile, using a whisk, beat the egg yolks with the sugar in a bowl for a couple of minutes or until the mixture becomes pale yellow. Only add the sugar to the yolks when you are ready to beat them: leaving the sugar to rest on the yolks may create lumps that are difficult to dissolve later. Sift the cornflour and salt into the whipped yolks and combine thoroughly.

3. When the milk starts simmering, remove from the heat and pour a ladleful through a sieve into the egg mixture and incorporate fully. The sieve is only needed if lemon peel has been added; for the chocolate and coffee versions, the sieving may be omitted. Pour the rest of the milk through the sieve into the egg mixture in 2 batches and combine. Discard the lemon peel.

4. Pour the warm mixture back into the milk pan and return to the heat, on a very low setting. Cook for 4–6 minutes, stirring continuously with a wooden spoon, until the mixture thickens. A wooden spoon is better than a whisk or a spatula: this way you can feel if the cream starts to stick to the bottom of the pan. If it does so, take it off the heat temporarily, reduce the heat if necessary and stir thoroughly and continuously when returning to the heat. Over time, the cream will change from a liquid into a thicker, creamy state passing through a lumpy phase: this is normal, just keep stirring vigorously and the texture will eventually homogenise. Remove from the heat at the first sign of boiling.

5. Let cool for 10 minutes, stirring occasionally to avoid forming a skin. Pour into a cold bowl, line the surface with clingfilm and set aside to cool completely. If not using straight away, store, lined with clingfilm, in the fridge for up to 5 days.

TIP

The cream will thicken significantly upon cooling, so you will need to beat it energetically to recover the creaminess before you can pipe it or spread it. If you are planning to pipe the cream, transfer it to the piping bag while still warm, pinching both ends

of the bag with plastic clips, and let it chill in the fridge until ready to use.

ALSO TRY...

ORANGE PASTRY CREAM

Add 100g (scant ½ cup) freshly squeezed orange juice to the warm mixture in step 4, once it has been returned to the heat. Do not pour the orange juice directly into the milk or it will curdle. Add the grated zest of the orange to the cream as soon as it is off the heat in step 5. For a more pungent flavour, also add ½ teaspoon of natural orange extract. For an alcoholic kick, add 2 tablespoons triple sec liqueur while the cream is still warm.

CHOCOLATE PASTRY CREAM

Omit the lemon peel, use 30g (⅓ cup) cornflour instead of 50g (½ cup), and add 80g (2¾oz) dark chocolate chips (50–55% cocoa solids) as soon as it is off the heat in step 5, stirring well to incorporate the chocolate. For a more adult taste, add 2 tablespoons of rum to the warm cream, or, better still, 2 tablespoons of coffee liqueur. You will not be able to taste coffee, but it will add a warm and rich depth to the flavour.

COFFEE PASTRY CREAM

Omit the lemon peel. Add 2 tablespoons of soluble coffee to the hot milk in step 3 and mix until fully dissolved before incorporating the milk. If you prefer a sweeter cream, use 125g (⅔ cup) sugar instead of 110g (scant ⅔ cup). For a moreish boozy kick, add 2 tablespoons of sambuca to the cream while it is still warm.

Crema al Pistacchio
Pistachio Cream

gluten-free

MAKES ABOUT 700ML (24FL OZ)

For the pistachio butter
200g (1⅓ cups) whole, unsalted, blanched, skinned and roasted pistachio kernels (see pages 12–13)

For the cream
500g (2 cups) whole milk
1 tsp vanilla bean paste
75g (2½oz) egg yolk (about 5 medium egg yolks)
110g (scant ⅔ cup) caster (superfine) sugar
40g (scant ½ cup) cornflour (cornstarch)
small pinch of salt
80g (⅓ cup) pistachio butter

If the hazelnut is the king of nuts in northern Italy, pistachio undoubtedly takes the equivalent crown in southern Italy. The variety harvested in the city of Bronte, in Sicily, and surrounding areas is protected by Italian food law for its unrivalled quality. A trip to Sicily is guaranteed to offer you options to taste this very versatile nut in sweet as well as savoury preparations; it can even be made into a delicious pasta sauce!

Crema al pistacchio is a simple variation of the basic pastry cream opposite, prepared using the same method, with just the addition of a couple of spoonfuls of pistachio butter at the very end, so the tips for the basic cream recipe apply here too.

The flavour of *crema al pistacchio* is so intense that this, more than any other variant of cream, can be served as a dessert in its own right. It will make a very stylish entry to your dinner party if served in medium shot glasses, decorated with chocolate chips or chopped pistachios. If you have any available, pair it with dried edible rose petals: both the colour and the flavour combination are spectacular.

Buying the pistachio butter ready-made is the simplest option, as long as the butter is made with 100% nuts with no added oils, fats or sugars. However, pistachio butter is so simple (and much cheaper) to make at home that I always prepare my own, even though my domestic food processor might be unable to produce as smooth a butter as the industrial counterpart. Unsalted pistachio kernels are available in most supermarkets but bulk-buying them online makes this recipe more cost effective.

Typically, pistachio kernels are sold whole, and before they can be turned into butter, they must be skinned and slightly roasted. The process for skinning and roasting pistachios is quite simple and explained on pages 12–13.

This recipe will make more pistachio butter than needed to flavour a batch of pastry cream; however, the leftovers can be stored in a sealed glass jar in the fridge for up to 2 weeks and used later as a tasty spread or to flavour ice cream, smoothies, creams and cakes.

The amounts given will produce enough pistachio cream for one *torta della nonna* (pages 23–5), one batch of *pasticciotti* (pages 113–15), or one layer of filling in a 23–25cm (9–10in) round cake. To fill the celebration cake (pages 72–8), which requires two layers of cream, use about 1½ times the quantities above, while to fill a set of 12 *zeppole* (pages 127–31), double the amounts.

MAKE THE PISTACHIO BUTTER

1. If you are skinning and/or roasting the pistachios at home, ensure that they have cooled to room temperature (see pages 12–13).
2. Blitz the pistachios in a food processor on full speed; the butter is ready when all the pistachios have been crushed to a thick, smooth pulp. It will take about 3 minutes. Scrape the sides of the food processor bowl with a silicone spatula midway through the process to ensure that there are no coarse bits of nuts left over. Store any leftovers in a sealed glass jar in the fridge and use them within 2 weeks.

MAKE THE CREAM

3. Place the milk and vanilla in a pan and gently bring to a simmer. Meanwhile, beat the egg yolks with the sugar in a bowl using a whisk for a couple of minutes or until the mixture becomes pale yellow. Sift the cornflour and salt into the yolks and combine thoroughly.
4. As soon as the milk starts simmering, remove from the heat and pour a ladleful into the egg mixture and incorporate fully. Pour in the rest of the milk in 2 batches and combine.
5. Pour the warm mixture back into the milk pan and return to a very low heat. Cook for 4–6 minutes, stirring continuously with a wooden spoon, until the mixture thickens. Remove from the heat at the first sign of boiling.
6. Place the pistachio butter in a small bowl and add a few tablespoons of warm cream, one at a time, incorporating the cream into the butter well before subsequent additions. This step is needed to loosen the pistachio butter. If the pistachio butter is added directly to the cream, it might not dissolve and remain lumpy.
7. Add the cream/pistachio mixture to the rest of the cream and mix well until fully combined. Pour into a cold bowl, cover the surface of the cream with clingfilm and leave in the fridge to chill. If not using straight away, store, lined with clingfilm, in the fridge for up to 5 days.

ALSO TRY...

For an alcoholic kick, add 2 tablespoons of rum to the cold cream. Avoid adding it to the warm cream, as most of the alcohol will evaporate.

Crema al Gianduia
Gianduia Cream

MAKES ABOUT 700ML (24FL OZ)

For the hazelnut butter (makes 200g/7oz)
200g (1½ cups) whole, roasted and
    skinned hazelnuts (see pages 12–13)

For the cream
400g (1¾ cups) whole milk
1 tsp vanilla bean paste
60g (2¼oz) egg yolk (about 4 egg yolks)
100g (generous ½ cup) caster (superfine) sugar
30g (2 tbsp) cornflour (cornstarch)
small pinch of salt
40g (1½oz/¼ cup) dark chocolate chips or bar,
    broken into pieces (50–55% cocoa solids)
60g (¼ cup) hazelnut butter

Gianduia is the confectionery masterpiece of
Turin: it is a cream based on a blend of cocoa
and locally sourced hazelnuts, which were
introduced to the chocolate recipe in the early
19th century as a partial substitute for cocoa, to
address its rising cost. Chocolatiers in the Turin
area had access to very high-quality hazelnuts,
conveniently cultivated in Piedmont, and put
them to very good use coming up with one of
the most successful flavour combinations in the
confectionery world.

Crema al gianduia is a variation of the
basic pastry cream based on such a flavour
combination: high-quality chocolate chips are
melted in hot cream and a generous amount of
hazelnut butter is added to the mix. The result is
an indulgent, rich, but not overly sweet cream.
To ensure success, make sure that you follow
the hints and tips provided in the method for
making the basic pastry cream (pages 204–6).

Hazelnut butter can be bought ready-made,
but making it at home is deceptively simple and
only requires a good food processor, so why
not give it a try? Roast and skin the nuts first,
in order to achieve a finer butter texture (see
pages 12–13 for guidance).

This recipe will make more hazelnut butter
than needed for the cream, but leftovers can be
safely stored in the fridge for up to 2 weeks and
used later as a spread, drizzled over ice cream,
to flavour creams, biscuits or cakes.

The amounts given will produce enough
cream for one *torta della nonna* (pages 23–5),
one batch of *pasticciotti* (pages 113–15), or one
layer of filling in a 23–25cm (9–10in) round cake.
To fill the celebration cake (pages 72–8), which
requires two layers of cream, use about 1½
times the quantities above, while to fill a set of
12 *zeppole* (pages 127–31), double the amounts.

MAKE THE HAZELNUT BUTTER

1. If you are skinning and/or roasting the
   hazelnuts at home, ensure that they have
   cooled to room temperature (see pages 12–13).
2. Blitz the hazelnuts in a food processor on
   full speed; the butter is ready when all the
   hazelnuts have been crushed to an oily,
   smooth pulp. It will take about 2 minutes.
3. Scrape the sides of the food processor bowl
   with a silicone spatula midway through the
   process to ensure that there are no coarse
   bits of nuts left over. Do not overwork the
   butter and stop the food processor as soon
   as possible to avoid overheating the nuts.
   Store any leftovers in a sealed glass jar in
   the fridge and use within 2 weeks.

MAKE THE CREAM

4. Place the milk and vanilla in a pan and gently bring to a simmer. Meanwhile, beat the egg yolks with the sugar in a bowl using a whisk for a couple of minutes or until the mixture becomes pale yellow. Sift the cornflour and salt into the yolks and combine thoroughly.

5. As soon as the milk starts simmering, remove from the heat and pour a ladleful into the egg mixture and incorporate fully. Pour the rest of the milk into the egg mixture in 2 batches and combine.

6. Pour the warm mixture back into the milk pan and return to the heat, on a very low setting. Cook for 4–6 minutes, stirring continuously with a wooden spoon, until the mixture thickens. Remove from the heat at the first sign of boiling.

7. Let cool for a couple of minutes and then add the chocolate chips (or chocolate pieces), stirring to incorporate the chocolate. While still warm, add the hazelnut butter and mix well until fully combined. Pour into a cold bowl, cover the surface of the cream with clingfilm and leave in the fridge to chill. If not using straight away, store, lined with clingfilm, in the fridge for up to 5 days.

ALSO TRY…

For an alcoholic kick, add 2 tablespoons of rum to the cold cream. Avoid adding it to the warm cream, as most of the alcohol will evaporate.

Pasta Sfoglia
Puff Pastry

— egg-free
— nut-free

MAKES 1.25KG (2LB 12OZ)

For the *pastello*
360g (2¾ cups) plain (all-purpose) flour,
    plus extra for dusting
200g (scant 1 cup) cold water
1½ tsp salt

For the *panetto*
200g (1½ cups) plain (all-purpose) flour
500g (2¼ cups) unsalted butter, cold

Puff pastry is a very versatile basic pastry with origins dating back several centuries; however, the version that we all know and love was standardised in France in the 18th century. From there, it was exported almost everywhere in Europe; in fact, many traditional Italian bakes nowadays, both sweet and savoury, use a base of puff pastry or *pasta sfoglia*. Although the preparation does require a bit of patience, it is worth practising, as the end result is distinctly better than any shop-bought alternative.

The list of ingredients for *pasta sfoglia* is remarkably short; it is, in fact, all in the method! Do not be put off, however, by the apparently complex description: the process is not difficult; it is actually simpler to do than to describe. It may look long, but the majority is resting time requiring little or no action.

The all-essential layers in *pasta sfoglia* are produced by alternating a lean component, the *pastello* (made with flour, water and salt), with a fat component, the *panetto* (made with flour and butter). The main pitfall that must be avoided at all costs is the butter melting, therefore, do not skip the chilling steps and

avoid making *pasta sfoglia* on the hottest day of the year.

The following recipe produces a generous batch of *pasta sfoglia*: it's worth making enough to last you for 2–3 bakes. It stores well in the fridge for up to 4–5 days and can be frozen for up to a month, then thawed when needed, so no part of it will be wasted.

1. Take the butter out of the fridge and dice it into 2cm (¾in) cubes. Set it aside to warm up slightly.

MAKE THE PASTELLO

2. Add the flour, water and salt to the bowl of a stand mixer fitted with the dough hook and start the mixer on medium speed. Knead the dough for about 4 minutes until it looks smooth and comes cleanly off the sides of the bowl. If the quantity of dough is too little for the mixer attachment to work it properly, knead it by hand. Shape the *pastello* into a 15cm (6in) square, wrap it in clingfilm and leave it to rest in the fridge.

MAKE THE PANETTO

3. Meanwhile, prepare the *panetto* by adding the flour and the diced butter to the same stand mixer bowl used for the *pastello*. Start the mixer (still fitted with the dough hook) on low speed first, then increase to medium. Work the mixture until there are no lumps of butter left. Scrape the sides of the bowl with a spatula once or twice to ensure that all the butter is evenly mixed with the flour. Once

the mixture has come together, drop it on to a sheet of baking paper. It will be soft and very sticky, so avoid touching it or handling it with bare hands: instead, cover the *panetto* with a second sheet of baking paper and carefully shape it into a 20cm (8in) square, about 2cm (¾in) thick. Leave the *panetto*, still wrapped in baking paper, to chill in the fridge for at least 15 minutes or until stiff.

MAKE THE PASTRY

4. While the *panetto* chills, take the *pastello* out of the fridge (keep the clingfilm so you can re-use it later), lightly dust the worktop with flour and roll it into a 30cm (12in) square with a rolling pin. Try to keep the shape as square as possible, moulding the corners and straightening up the sides by hand or with the help of a long knife, if necessary.
5. Take the *panetto* out of the fridge, remove the baking paper and place it in the middle of the *pastello*, with the sides at a 45° angle with the sides of the *pastello*. Fold the 4 corners of the *pastello* over the sides of the *panetto* to enclose it completely and so that the corners of the *pastello* meet neatly in the centre. Pinch together the edges of the adjacent sides of the *pastello* to enclose the *panetto* fully (see page 215).
6. Gently roll the parcel of pastry to a thickness of 8–10mm (⅜–½in) to form a rectangle with the long side facing you. Fold the left third over the centre, then fold the right third over the centre (see pages 214–15). You have completed the first fold. Before each folding step, brush the excess flour off the top of the pastry with a clean, dry pastry brush.

7. Rotate the folded parcel by 90°, so that one of the two folded ends is now facing you, roll it again to a thickness of 8–10mm (⅜–½in) and form a rectangle. Repeat the folding as previously to complete the second fold. Wrap the pastry in the clingfilm you saved earlier and leave it to rest in the fridge for 30 minutes. (Scan the QR code for a video tutorial.)
8. Once the pastry has chilled, take it out of the fridge, save the clingfilm, place it on the floured worktop with one folded end facing you and repeat steps 6 and 7 twice more to perform a total of 6 folds. After completing the last fold, leave the pastry to chill in the fridge for at least 2 hours before using it. If not using straight away, store, wrapped in clingfilm, in the fridge for up to 5 days or freeze for up to a month.

ALSO TRY...

If I am in a hurry, I find that 4 folds are usually sufficient to produce a decently layered pastry, however, nothing beats the flakiness and lightness of a fully formed puff pastry. Nevertheless, I recommend not exceeding 6 folds to avoid compromising the stability of the layering altogether.

Scan here to see how to fold *pastello* and *panetto* to make *pasta sfoglia*.

GIUSEPPE'S ITALIAN BAKES

Zabaione

— gluten-free
— dairy-free
— nut-free

MAKES ABOUT 250ML (9FL OZ)

90g (3¼oz) egg yolk (about 6 medium egg yolks)
80g (scant ½ cup) caster (superfine) sugar
80g (⅓ cup) dry Marsala wine

Zabaione is a very rich, traditional and versatile custard-like preparation, made with a base of egg yolk, sugar and a sweet wine, roughly in the same quantities. There are as many theories about its origin as there are variations of the basic recipe. Sweetness can be adjusted by modifying the amount of sugar and the final thickness can be controlled by adding more or less wine to produce either a pourable custard or a creamy, eggnog-like drink.

To obtain a thickness suitable for filling *cannoncini* (pages 125–6), halve the amount of wine.

Preparation is easy, but to reach the all-important silky smooth texture, keep whisking the egg mixture over the bain-marie continuously and steadily, taking it off the heat as soon as it reaches 80°C (176°F): scrambled eggs are just around the corner...

A bit of a warning: steer clear of *zabaione* if you are not a fan of very rich and sweet creams; on the other hand, if you are after an energy kick, this will certainly give you all the calories you need!

1. Prepare a bain-marie by bringing 2.5cm (1in) of water to a gentle simmer in a pan.
2. Add the egg yolks and sugar to a metal bowl and beat with a handheld electric whisk on high speed for 4–5 minutes until pale and fluffy.

3. Add the Marsala wine to the egg mixture and move the metal bowl over the pan with the simmering water. Immediately reduce the setting to the lowest possible heat. Keep whisking vigorously and steadily with a hand whisk until the temperature reaches 80°C (176°F). If you do not have a thermometer, a good sign that the egg is cooked is that the mixture is no longer liquid, and the whisk will leave marks that do not disappear. Remove the bowl from the bain-marie and keep whisking until the *zabaione* is completely cool.
4. If you are not using it immediately, pour the *zabaione* into a cold bowl (preferably a wide glass bowl or a ceramic tray) and line the surface with clingfilm. Store, lined with clingfilm, in the fridge for up to 3 days.

ALSO TRY...

The traditional recipe calls for Marsala, but any sweet wine, such as vin santo or Moscato d'Asti, will do. For a stronger version, use rum instead. Spices such as cinnamon or nutmeg are ideal additions during the Christmas period, while fresh, acidic berries are excellent to cut through the richness and sweetness of *zabaione*.

Pasta Frolla

MAKES ABOUT 850G (1LB 14OZ)

400g (4 cups) soft wheat 00 flour
200g (scant 1 cup) cold unsalted butter, diced
140g (1 cup) icing (confectioners') sugar
100g (3½oz) egg (about 2 medium eggs), cold
zest of 1 organic lemon
1 tsp vanilla bean paste
⅛ tsp salt

Pasta frolla literally means 'crumbly pastry', and is one of the pillars of Italian baking. Like a sweet shortcrust pastry, it is simple yet deliciously short, and is used in many biscuits, cakes, pies and tarts.

There are many versions of this recipe, some of which ask you to cream the butter and sugar together. However, this version uses a tried and tested method that prevents the flour from forming a glutinous network, allowing the pastry to retain its perfect, crumbly texture, and it hasn't failed me yet. The key is to keep the mixture – and especially the butter – as cold as you can.

Avoid overworking the dough to ensure you end up with a very crumbly, almost creamy texture. The very first sheet of *pasta frolla* you produce will have the best texture. Any leftovers can be baked as simple but delicious biscuits. Re-roll to a thickness of 3mm (⅛in) or 5mm (¼in) and bake for 8–12 minutes, depending on thickness.

1. If possible, chill the flour in the freezer for 30 minutes before using it as it will help keep the mixture cold. Place the flour in a large bowl and add the butter. Work the mixture by pinching the pieces of butter with the tips of your fingers to break them into very small lumps, fully coated in flour. Keep working the mixture quickly (without crushing it) until it resembles fine, loose breadcrumbs.
2. Make a well in the sandy mixture and add the remaining ingredients. Mix in the egg and sugar with your hands first, then gradually incorporate the flour mixture by scooping it up from the bottom of the bowl and folding it over, rather than crushing it together: this will create large, well-separated flakes of pastry.
3. Turn the mixture on to the worktop, flatten it with the palms of your hands and fold it in half. Repeat the flattening and folding no more than 3–4 times until the dough forms a roughly homogeneous mass. The dough will be sticky, so a metal scraper will be of great help here.
4. Flatten the dough, wrap it in clingfilm and chill in the fridge for at least 30 minutes, better still for a couple of hours. Resting in the fridge is a critical part of making *pasta frolla* as its texture dramatically changes when the butter hardens in the cold fridge, making it much less sticky and easier to manage and shape. If not using straight away, store, wrapped in clingfilm, in the fridge for up to 3 days or freeze for up to a month.

vegan
egg-free
dairy-free
nut-free

Grano Cotto
Cooked Wheat Grain

MAKES 600G (1LB 5OZ)

200g (1¼ cups) raw wheat grain

Cooked wheat grain is an essential ingredient of *pastiera* (pages 33–6). It is sold ready-made in jars or cans all over Italy, but it can be trickier to find abroad. Nevertheless, it can be made at home from raw wheat grain, which is easier to source. The process does not require much effort, but it is lengthy: it requires 3 days of soaking, a couple of hours' cooking and an overnight cooling; start at least 4 days before the cooked wheat grain is needed.

The wheat grain will almost triple in weight upon cooking, if the recipe calls for 300g (10½oz) cooked wheat grain, you should start with 100g (3½oz) raw grain. However, I would recommend always cooking at least twice the minimum quantity, just in case: the leftover cooked grain is an excellent addition to salads, and it can replace couscous or rice in hot and cold dishes.

1. On day 1, wash the raw wheat grain thoroughly in plenty of cold water. If husks come floating to the surface, skim them off and discard. Drain and place in a large bowl. Cover with plenty of cold, clean water – at least twice the volume of the wheat – and leave it to soak. You will notice the grain just starting to swell slightly during the first 24 hours.
2. On days 2 and 3, drain the grain, rinse it under running water, then place it back in the bowl and cover it with fresh clean water. It does not look like much is happening, but this stage is critical to allow thorough cooking.
3. On day 4, drain and rinse the grain one last time, place it in a large pan and pour in 3–4 times its volume in boiling water. Partially cover the pan, ideally by wedging a wooden spoon under the lid, so that steam can escape but the heat is retained.
4. Simmer over a very low heat for 1½–2 hours, topping up with boiling water to ensure the grain does not dry out. Cooking time varies significantly, depending on the type, size and nature of the wheat grain: I have used grains that took up to 3 hours to cook, so be patient and do not rush this stage. The grain is fully cooked when all grains are cracked open and noticeably swollen: the fleshy white core should bloom out of the darker skin and, most importantly, when pinched between your fingertips, they should have the texture of cooked pulses.
5. Remove the pan from the heat, cover it and leave the grain to cool completely, still in the cooking water, ideally overnight.
6. On day 5, drain the grain in a colander and rinse it well under cold, running water. You might notice a gelatinous liquid around the grain, this is normal, and will easily rinse off. Leave the grain in the colander over a tray or a bowl for at least 30 minutes to drain fully. Your wheat grain is now ready to use: it will keep in the fridge for no more than 2-3 days.

Index

Managing Director Sarah Lavelle

Editor Vicky Orchard

Head of Design Claire Rochford

Designer Studio Polka

Senior Commissioning Editor Sophie Allen

Assistant Editor Sofie Shearman

Photographer Matt Russell

Food Stylists Jack Sargeson and Troy Willis

Prop Stylist Rachel Vere

Head of Production Stephen Lang

Senior Production Controller Lisa Fiske

First published in 2022 by Quadrille,
an imprint of Hardie Grant Publishing

Quadrille
52–54 Southwark Street
London SE1 1UN
quadrille.com

Text © Giuseppe Dell'Anno 2022
Photography © Matt Russell 2022
Design and layout © Quadrille 2022

Cataloguing in Publication Data: a catalogue record
for this book is available from the British Library.

9781787139282
Printed in China

Grazie!

Writing this book has truly been a family affair: first and foremost, I must thank my better half Laura for tolerating me when I was at my most insufferable; thanks to my sweet great-auntie Vera for her masterclasses; thanks to my precious mother-in-law Giuseppina for her constant supply of *pucce*; thanks to my cousins Vincenzo e Viviana for their priceless support, and thanks to Floriana who, although not a part of the family, I have known for so long that it is almost as if she were.

Thanks to papà for being such an inspiration, a truly wonderful human being and the best role model ever, and thanks to mamma for devoting herself to him now that he needs her most.

Thanks to Vivienne, Sarah and the whole team at Quadrille for supporting a clueless novice all the way through, and thanks to Jack, Troy and Rachel for styling my bakes in the most mouth-watering way. Thanks to Matt for being a joy to work with and for skilfully elevating my food (and, miraculously, my ugly face) with his breathtaking photos.

And, finally, thank you all for encouraging me throughout this journey and for showing some interest in this book. I will be forever grateful!